W9-DDT-677

THE WORLD IS A PRISON

THE
WORLD
IS A
PRISON

GUGLIELMO PETRONI

TRANSLATED FROM THE ITALIAN BY JOHN SHEPLEY

TMP THE MARLBORO PRESS / NORTHWESTERN
NORTHWESTERN UNIVERSITY PRESS
EVANSTON, ILLINOIS

The Marlboro Press/Northwestern
Northwestern University Press
Evanston, Illinois 60208-4210

Originally published in Italian under the title *Il mondo è una prigione.* Copyright
© 1996 by Giunte Gruppo Editoriale, Florence. English translation copyright
© 1999 by Northwestern University Press. Published 1999 by The Marlboro
Press/Northwestern. All rights reserved.

Printed in the United States of America

ISBN 0-8101-6050-1 (cloth)
ISBN 0-8101-6051-X (paper)

Library of Congress Cataloging-in-Publication Data

Petroni, Guglielmo, 1911–
    [Mondo è una prigione. English]
    The world is a prison / Guglielmo Petroni ; translated from the
Italian by John Shepley.
        p.   cm.
    ISBN 0-8101-6050-1. — ISBN 0-8101-6051-X (paper)
    1. Petroni, Guglielmo, 1911– . World War, 1939–1945—Prisoners
and prisons, Italian. 3. Prisoners of war—Italy Biography. I. Title.
D805.I8P48 1999
940.54'7245'092—dc21

                                                              99-27768
                                                                  CIP

The paper used in this publication meets the minimum requirements of the
American National Standard for Information Sciences—Permanence of Paper
for Printed Library Materials, ANSI Z39.48-1984.

Contents

Translator's Foreword

Guglielmo Petroni was born in 1911 in the small Tuscan city of Lucca. Though forced for economic reasons to leave school at an early age, he went on to become a poet and journalist in Florence and, after 1938, in Rome. In 1943 he joined the Resistance, and on 3 May 1944 was arrested with three companions; it is this experience of incarceration, beatings, and interrogations at the hands of the Fascists and Germans that forms the substance of *The World Is a Prison,* his most acclaimed book. After the war he resumed his literary career and published several novels, including *La casa si muove* (1949), *Noi dobbiamo parlare* (1955), *Il colore della terra* (1964), and *La morte del fiume,* which won the Premio Strega in 1974. His collected poems, written over a period of fifty years, were published as *Poesie* in 1978, and his autobiographical *Il nome delle parole* in 1984. He died in Rome in 1993.

Though in many ways a modest work, *The World Is a Prison* has shown remarkable staying power. First published in 1948 in the literary journal *Botteghe Oscure,* and the following year as a book by Mondadori, it has since been reprinted many times in Italy, most recently by Giunti in 1995. I say a modest work because of its unassuming tone, but it makes large claims and manages to live up to them. Petroni speaks for a generation of Italian intellectuals who came of age during the Fascist period, aware that they had been cheated of an important part of their heritage and uncertain as to how best to reclaim it.

In his opening chapters Petroni has some trenchant things to say about the stultifying provincial atmosphere in which he grew up, and it forms a backdrop to the thoughts and feelings that were to be crystallized by his prison experience. Yet, paradoxically, it was his feeling of isolation and estrangement that may have helped him to survive the ordeal. He is able to cultivate a kind of indifference, a protective shell that he takes to be instinctive, but which leaves his true feelings—and his powers of observation—unimpaired. It is a grim story, to be sure, but not without its comical moments, as when Petroni and his friends find themselves in a cell at the Mussolini Barracks with a pair of inept stool pigeons, or when his cellmates in the Via Tasso prison forcibly search his pockets for bits of tobacco.

Italy has a certain tradition of prison writing, which would include works written in prison and others later as memoirs after the writer was freed. One could conceivably go all the way back to Tommaso Campanella, the dissident Dominican friar, who in 1602 wrote his utopian treatise *Civitas Solis* (*The City of the Sun*) in the dungeons of the Inquisition. Closer to our own era is *Le mie prigioni* (*My Prisons*) by Silvio Pellico, published in 1832, an Italian patriot's account of his imprisonment by the Austrians in the Spielberg Fortress in Moravia. Its tone of Christian humility and resignation became irksome to later generations, but it remains a literary classic. In this century, Antonio Gramsci's prison letters and notebooks were a crucial source of inspiration for Italian writers and intellectuals after the Second World War; they exemplified a particular kind of heroism and testified to the existence of a critical, historically minded intelligence in the desert of Fascist times. Petroni, however, does not offer a blueprint for Utopia, Christian piety, or Marxist praxis—only the tortured and deprived human being, in relation to himself and others.

Italy's most famous modern prison survivor is, of course, Primo Levi. His account of his concentration-camp ordeal has spoken eloquently not only to Italy but to the world. The journalistic title *Survival in Auschwitz* was imposed on the English translation; the real title is *Se questo è un uomo* (*If This Is a Man*). And it is this same search for the meaning of humanity that Petroni's book implicitly shares, making it both part of an honorable tradition and a unique story of spiritual survival and growth.

J.S.

THE WORLD IS A PRISON

The World Is a Prison

Once again, as always, during one of my walks in the idle hours I now seldom spend in the city where I was born, at a certain point I went into the basilica of San Frediano. I know what took me there: childhood memories, the spell of a confused adolescence, the wish to renew an old fund of emotions and nostalgic feelings that come back all the more forcefully the more remote and buried they may seem.

It's a wholly automatic phenomenon. I can go back in that church as often as I like and, as though pressing a button to activate a sentimental mechanism, when I raise my eyes to the rugged architecture of the ceiling, plain, solemn, and perfect in its rustic geometry, the usual and ever-forgotten sensations well up again.

But once this sort of intellectual game is played out, I move toward the side aisle and approach the baptismal font, which stands protected by its slender wrought-iron railing. Here it is no longer a question of a mechanism—before this timeworn object I feel I am in the presence of my faithful touchstone. The splendid, meager figures going round and round are the scale on which from time to time I weigh the most recent passages in my life; it is a simple set of relations that I can establish immediately without thinking about it. As I draw near these marvelous figures, which never refuse to tell me, crudely and with the vehemence of primitive spirits, about their centuries of life and how they're condemned to go on signifying until their marble is consumed by time, I recognize, by the renewed sensation I get from them, what recent experiences of my own are fated to leave a mark on my existence.

This time as well, slowly, with the fervid indolence I can draw on in the lost and heedless hours I spend in my city—vacation hours, remote from the doggedness of living and surviving—I made the circuit of those few meters of marble.

It is a baptismal font quite well known in art history. Erected in the twelfth century, or perhaps the thirteenth, it is attributed to the Master of the San Frediano Font and Master Roberto. Biduino may also have worked on it, and this name utterly charms me by its barbaric ring. In addition to the corporeal image of God, there are the carved figures of Pharaoh's soldiers crossing the Red Sea, with the waters beginning to lap at the hooves of their horses and fish disporting themselves in the waves. The horses are nervous, with the proud, clear-cut heads of racetrack thoroughbreds; the fishes leap from one ripple to another; and the riders, petrified in their saddles, are all wrong in their joints, with their feet often pointed in a direction contrary to anatomical logic. Then there are many silent characters from the Old Testament and the humble Good Shepherd, the romantic young socialist of the times when people's minds were as yet untroubled by either socialism or romanticism, but were intent instead on the abstract unknown of human consciousness.

This time I was especially drawn to the figure of a man with a broken face, encumbered by a toga that had never been ironed, and struggling with a monster with the body and claws of a rooster, a crocodile's tail, a serpent's neck, and the head of a cat. The enraged man has seized the horrible tail, while the rooster turns its feline head on its serpent's neck with motionless and age-old fury.

No need to indulge in rhetoric in my silent colloquy with this lucidly carved group: it was enough to be vaguely aware of countless meanings touching my recent existence, which, as never before, had been like that of many other people. The struggle with the horrifying composite monster was easy to understand—the whole world was still struggling with it.

On leaving the church, I went to the bar on the opposite corner, as I've done for years. With that vast and resonant gloom behind me, I felt hundreds of years old, old as all the men of my land, my shoulders drooping under all that arduous and profound past. I was oppressed, chained by my civilization, which I often hate and hated all the more at that moment, since once again my heart was swelling in vain—in vain, as I've known ever since I was born. Standing near me at the counter in the bar were two young American G.I.'s, who had drunk a good deal more than what was allowed to the survivors of Prohibition.

"Cigarette?" said one, extending the pack to me.

"No." But then I accepted it.

After a while, almost falling down drunk: "You know signorina? You introduce me to signorina?"

"No."

"Why no?"

"Because no!" I answered with some vehemence.

I turned away. A few minutes went by, then he took a swing at me, but since drunks have trouble gauging distance he didn't hit me, and all I felt was a swoosh of air from his big fist. I knew that a tacit Anglo-Saxon code of mutual respect permitted only a response in kind; indeed, I have the greatest esteem for the chivalry of an age that counsels such behavior and has already had an impact on a nation that the world associates with the stiletto. But I responded the way Anglo-Saxons think only a Negro would respond—with a kick—which didn't reach the worthy fellow only because he was drunk and unsteady on his feet. Yes, like a Negro! I had by now emerged from the silent and oppressive conversation with the whole past afflicting our existence, I was still soaked up to my neck in our decayed experience, I was unbelievably old. Better that barbarous violence, that bastard gesture so in contrast to my entire self, than the courtly condescension, timeworn and indifferent, urged on me by the ten centuries to which I, almost drunk myself, went back.

Yes, like a Negro! Better that way, never mind why. But it certainly wasn't because of these two nice guys who were having fun drinking and thinking about girls. Besides, it may not have been for nothing that Biduino had been among those to drive his chisel into the wonderful marbles whose luminous image was still before my eyes.

I left the place followed by the skeptical smiles of three old fellow townsmen, who watched me placidly and with indifference over their glasses of wine, and by the cheerful, childish benevolence of the two G.I.'s.

Again I walked through the dark streets, assailed by a raw irritation with the world. Though I didn't recognize it at once, it didn't take long to identify—it was the same feeling that had often befallen me of late, the one that had come over me in the confused moments of my recent existence.

I had suddenly had this feeling of dismay seven months earlier, at a time when an experience that had made all the most striking features of my past look ephemeral was coming to an end. The first occasion was at the moment of emerging from the darkness of the German prison on Via Tasso in Rome, but just then I still had too many immediate worries. I was about to leave one dreadful place for another one like it, where the near future was even darker and more uncertain, and so I had no chance to stop and analyze what I felt. There was no opportunity to ask myself what this regret meant, this sorrow at leaving a place where, along with others, I would slowly have died. But on 4 June, as I left the prison of Regina Cœli, truly free at last, and set out for the Lungotevere della Lungara, I had time to mull over this kind of spiritual dismay that was attacking me for the second time. I had stopped for a moment outside the prison gate, anticipating the sigh of relief that swells your chest when you come back to life and again see people and the sky, having almost lost them forever. I had raised my eyes to the city's rooftops; the sky, the sky of Rome, was perfect; but my chest swelled only with a deep regret, a peculiar and perhaps confused regret. I realized I was frantically mourning the hours when my life hung in the balance, threatened at every turn; I was mourning hunger, darkness, uncertainty, all the things that this time I was finally leaving behind.

I was footloose once more on the streets of Rome, or rather *free* for the first time. I was going back among people, some of whom even loved me, with a bundle full of rags and bedbugs under my arm; I was part of the movement of the streets, there was the sun and sky, and the trees were still putting forth fresh leaves. I had escaped death, uncertainty, fear—how could I not be happy? I should have been and wanted to be, but the sense of deception persisted. I was walking in the excited crowd, the last Germans were fleeing with grim faces, their weapons lowered, but in my heart I felt the growing difficulty of returning to my fellow humans. I felt the strongest attraction to the days spent in the filthy cells of the prisons I had known in those few weeks, which seemed like years.

So are prison and freedom not real prison, real freedom? May not the world itself be a prison? May not we ourselves be our prison, or else is our freedom only in ourselves? Are others perhaps your prison? A prison you may be able to love, as now you love that pile of concrete you're leaving behind with this obscure regret?

Later I even found explanations for this psychological process, and I understood the romantic nature of this sentiment. I thought I had explained it to myself, but I never ceased to feel that all my reasoning was in vain, that certain truths of our minds have a meaning that is needlessly profaned every time we try to strip it of its mystery.

Anyway, from that day on I felt closer to other people. I loved more consciously those I had loved in the past by instinct and choice but had neglected in life; I drew closer to those who were suffering in a world devastated by war, and not only by war.

That irritation with existence, however, the boredom of living with others, attacked me at various times when I least expected it. Often it seemed to me that therein lay the whole meaning of my more refined and intellectual past: there was an I who had been driven out by events, and who now took his revenge by these obscure and mournful assaults.

Upward and Onward

Time slipped by and the war continued at a slow pace, while I waited for my city to be liberated, so as to be able to go back immediately and see my family, my home, all the places I had never gone so long without seeing. When it finally happened, I tried to leave Rome, but no one was allowed to. I waited as long as I could, then set out one day without "permission," and with no idea how I'd get there. I started out on foot, a journey I had so often made in the warmth and comfort of a dining car on the train.

People planted themselves along the highways and begged rides from the truck drivers. An unusual sort of benevolence had emerged, however; perhaps the countless wayfarers lost in the middle of the countryside had always such desperate looks on their faces that no driver with the slightest sensitivity had the nerve to pass without trying to alleviate their distress.

As far as Civitavecchia there was a kind of milk train that one needed permission to board; but the conductor looked me in the eye, nodded his head, and ended by issuing me a ticket with a fine, then moved on without bothering about me anymore.

Night was already falling, the first night of my trip, when I found myself, along with four soldiers and a navy lieutenant, at the foot of the hill of Tarquinia. I thus came to know the little town that seemed to me the oldest place I had ever seen. We spent part of the night in the town's taverns, where a large number of displaced persons like ourselves wandered in and out; later we found the "hotel," a large peasants' house. I slept near the huge kitchen, where for half the night a numerous family who seemed earthlike and baked by the sun, just like the terra-cottas of their age-old ancestors, cracked nuts with a hammer, at an infuriating and mysterious pace, almost until dawn. It was as though they were performing a monotonous, primitive task that had been going on for centuries.

In the morning we were back on the Via Aurelia, where at every turn shabby Italian soldiers, haggard from sleepless nights, joined me and other tired "civilians" in begging a ride in any motor vehicle that went by. Christmas was coming and almost all these soldiers were on leave after many years of service, of sad wars and painful adventures that made no sense to them. They were the flotsam and jetsam of the war that had passed through these parts several months before. And yet these innocent human beings, resigned, jostled about at the edges of a hundred battles, oppressed by horrors and outrageous miscalculations, still kept something of life, something that preserved their sensitivity. Tirelessly, with faith and perseverance, fearfully stubborn, they were searching for their last ties with life, something to justify an existence the memory of which they had almost lost. They were returning to their villages, their homes, often without knowing whether those homes and villages still existed, or if even the people with whom they had begun their lives existed.

I did not consider myself unlike them in any way, and I got along well with them, preferring them to the civilians. They, however, looked on me as a creature apart. I was aware of it from the beginning. Among other things, I was properly dressed, and I had a suitcase, which suggested something of family life, a bourgeois existence they did not even remember, though they could still instinctively recognize its signs.

But this apparent difference didn't matter; since I felt I was one of them, it was easily overcome by an identity of sentiments. Indeed, every time I fell in behind a little group of soldiers, after a moment or two I was almost always able, unwittingly, to gain their sympathy and share in their terms the fate of a displaced person on the highway.

I arrived in Grosseto two days before Christmas; despite my hopes, on Christmas morning I was still in Livorno. I had got that far in three days thanks to the benevolent, even fond welcome of the polite, curly-haired inhabitants of central Italy, who foreshadow the romantic and tempestuous southerners, and thanks to the generosity of the drivers, those demigods of the highway on whom, when they stop for you, a displaced person alone or with companions in misfortune, beside a ditch, you look with instinctive veneration, ready to place all your belongings, all your pride, at their feet. But I had not reckoned on the fact that I was now standing at the threshold of decayed Tuscany, the land of majestic Renaissance egoism, the land of men whose keen eyes shine with indifference and a passion for themselves. Each of them is an insurmountable world, and already has everything going for him.

Four days of experience had made me more adept at begging rides, but from dawn to noon not one truck or car had stopped. I decided to go into the city to find something to eat. In all the previous days on the road I had never failed to get lunch and supper regularly, but here, though I wandered around for three hours asking everybody, and offering to pay more and more, I found no one willing to part with a piece of bread. I was already beginning to feel the fatigue of three hectic days and, by four o'clock in the afternoon, still clutching my suitcase, I had done many kilometers without finding anything except some awful brandy, for which I'd paid an exorbitant price. It was Christmas; Livorno, now reduced by the bombings to the little quadrangle of a central quarter, teemed with people circulating Sunday fashion in the half-ruined streets. By now I felt exhausted, but had I stayed there I would certainly have greeted the hour of curfew lost in the rubble and at the mercy of the Allied military police, who, since the place was still a war zone, weren't overly particular about whom they arrested. So I decided to go on to Pisa and started off with the hope of finding two things: something in the countryside to relieve my hunger and at least a hayloft in which to spend the night.

Christmas or not, at the edges of the war the military traffic was dizzying. Hundreds and hundreds of huge vehicles went by with no letup; the traffic on the road to Pisa was deafening; the asphalt trembled under my feet. Once past Livorno you could feel the war; there was a wary, overheated behind-the-lines atmosphere in which you no longer met displaced persons on the road. I was alone, no longer consoled by frequent encounters with other tired travelers who, trusting to chance, desperate but stubborn, were all returning in search of their own people in places where the war had since passed. Now I was truly alone.

It was then I was struck by something I hadn't realized: my suitcase was heavy, and on the day I left Rome, rested and well fed, I could hardly walk a hundred yards without stopping to change hands. Now, tired and sleepy, I had already done several kilometers and was setting out to do another fifty on foot, lugging it along almost without noticing.

Mental recuperation has an effect on one's arms, I thought. After stopping for another swig of truly abominable brandy, I set out again on the road to Pisa. The road separating the Tuscan port from the old maritime city is largely uninhabited, and runs monotonously through an agricultural zone almost swampy in nature, at least on the inland side. On the other, you are aware of the sea, beyond the dense pine groves that rise and fall along a line of small natural hillocks.

I walked till it was almost dark. At every farmhouse I asked for bread, offering to pay as much as they wanted, but they scarcely answered, while giving me a look of suspicion that was more painful to me than hunger. The hunger I thought I had left behind in Via Tasso once again bore down on my existence, aggravated by fatigue. With every fresh effort to find something to eat I increased my offer, now displaying several hundred lire for a piece of bread, but they just looked at me and shook their heads when I offered them money; they sent me away with what to me looked like a malicious smile. They didn't need money; the war had even put some in their pockets, something that had seldom happened to them before, and this was enough to make them indifferent to the sufferings of others. No, it wasn't indifference; we were in Tuscany, the land where man suffers at seeing the sufferings of others, and the more he suffers, the more he immures himself in a vast egoism that keeps him from thinking how a relatively unselfish gesture might spare him the pain of witnessing the pains of others. But to Tuscans it would seem to be a good thing to suffer from the sufferings of others, with the conviction of having thereby exhausted all charity.

I kept on walking, at a slow and dogged pace. But when the air turned gray and the ground hardened under my chilled feet, while the water alongside the road froze solid under my heels, I stopped to look around.

I had done thirteen kilometers. On the side of the road toward the sea, clumps of pine trees writhed against the greenish sky; on the other, marshy fields almost immersed in darkness stretched away in silence as far as the distant hills.

The only place where I might have lain down, beneath the shoulder of the road, was covered with frozen puddles, and when I inspected it I realized that the slope of the terrain gave no shelter and the wind there was every bit as strong. After standing still for a few moments, I felt that a whole night in this cold would be enough to put an end to my weary journey. On the horizon was a house, one of those dull farmhouses consisting of two buildings connected by an open shed, which shelters the oxcart and a few piles of rubble.

I walked up to the door and knocked. When it opened, I wanted first of all to ask again for some bread, but too many refusals had left me so disheartened that all I asked for was a glass of water.

"We don't have much," the man said, as he went to get it for me.

"Do you have some place where I could sleep?" I asked, getting up my courage.

"No, we don't."

"The shed would be all right."

"You'd freeze to death by morning. I wouldn't advise it.

You can't stay there, try down the road. There's another house half an hour away."

I tried to keep walking, but it was now dark, my legs buckled, and I couldn't go on. I stopped for half an hour on the road, and that was enough for the cold literally to take possession of me.

So I went back, and without asking permission threw myself down on a pile of wet sedge in the shed. Even there the cold was just as raw as in the open, but I no longer had the strength to move; I was incapable of remembering or thinking about anything. At the open sides of the shed a splendid moon threw perfect shadows on the ground. Twenty minutes or so had gone by when the black silhouette of a dog appeared on the threshold a few yards away. He sniffed the air—he was big but to me he looked huge— lifted his muzzle, and barked furiously, then hurled himself on me, snarling, as I did my best to take refuge in the cart.

"Padrone! Padrone!" I yelled.

Two men came out immediately. They stopped in the icy moonlight and stood watching in silence.

"Call off the dog, please . . . I lay down here to sleep . . . he's trying to bite me!"

At last one of them called the dog, then, himself mad as the animal, came up to me. "What are you doing here? Don't you know enough to ask somebody's permission?"

"I asked your permission a while ago, when I came to drink a glass of water."

"Why didn't you go to the next house?"

"I couldn't make it."

"But here you'll freeze to death."

"I hope not."

They went back in the house without answering. I was

exhausted and lay down again on the pile of sedge. Soon the dog came back and jumped on me, more furious than ever; this time I hadn't the strength to climb up on the cart and tried to hold him off by using my suitcase as a shield. I yelled again, and now three peasants came out, grumbling. They stood lined up in front of the shed and called off the dog.

"You got an identity card?" one of them asked.

In a daze, I moved forward to hand it to him, but a few steps away from them everything went blank . . .

When I came to, I was lying on the ground at the same spot where I had fallen. A few moments must have passed, but the three men still stood there in a row, black against the moon, looking at me without speaking. It was the first time in my life I had fainted, something I found hard to account for; I staggered to my feet, but they didn't lift a hand or move a step toward me.

"I fell down," I said.

No one answered, much less budged, and I too kept silent. We stayed like that for a while, until one of them said, "Your identity card."

I found it on the ground, picked it up, and handed it to him, hardly knowing what I was doing. They took it in the house, and after a while came back to say, "We'll keep your identity card till tomorrow morning."

Whereupon the youngest one added, "Come along, I'll show you a place where it's not so cold."

I followed him, mumbling that I hadn't eaten for twenty-four hours, in the puerile hope that he'd offer me something. I must have whined like a child, explaining how I'd been walking for kilometers and kilometers, lugging my big suitcase, but he didn't answer. He traversed the barnyard, crossed a wooden footbridge, went up a hillock, then down to a canal. I followed him, and when he stopped I realized that, having moved a short distance from him, I was in water up to my ankles. "Inside this hole you won't feel the cold." Indeed, there was a hole in the bank, slightly above the level of the water.

"Goodnight," he said, as I tried to figure out how I was supposed to get inside the hole. "What time tomorrow morning do you want your identity card?"

"Eight o'clock," I answered, and it occurred to me that his question and my answer were the same dialogue that takes place in third-class hotels between the guest and the boy who carries the suitcases into the elevator.

The hole led to a kind of burrow hollowed out in the earth, perhaps three meters long and one high. At the back was a little damp straw; it was completely dark inside, and the entrance hole at my feet looked like a white spot. I don't know what I was feeling as I lay there: in addition to the oddness of the place, my hunger and fatigue, I must surely have had the sensation of being unable to connect my thoughts logically, remember what had happened in the previous hours, or have a clear idea of where I was. My first thoughts were of a grave; this idea, despite the fact I was awake, took possession of me like a frightful hallucination, or rather an agonizing reality. But slowly sleep began to immobilize all my limbs. I had the vague impression that life was about to abandon me, it was hard to breathe, and the air was oppressive.

Half an hour may have gone by and I had already lost any awareness of the place and of myself, perhaps I had already dozed off into a confused and restless sleep, when I was awakened by something new close by; with a start I heard it running wildly around me on the straw—there was an animal in the burrow. I sat up in terror. As long as I didn't move, there was silence; when I moved, the creature began bumping against the walls, running across the straw. This time it was terror, the kind of terror one can only feel as a child, but magnified and crazy. I held my head in my hands and thought that by morning my hair would have all turned white; something in my reason was cracking up. Imprisoned in that hole in the ground, exhausted, hounded, I somehow had the feeling I was experiencing the world the way a hunted wild animal does; it seemed to me that an absurd conflict was going on in my mind in trying to retain the sense of being a man while even physically I felt like a wolf. Out of all this came a vague terror and an aversion for humanity. I was rejected, cast into an eternal solitude, and unwittingly I was afraid I'd no longer be recognized by my fellow men. I don't know what happened next; when I opened my eyes again, it was broad daylight and I was alone in the burrow.

This must surely be how the starving wolf awakens, tired and numbed by cold and the dampness of the earth; in the same way, he is afraid of the new day and pauses at the threshold of his burrow, and it is with these same eyes that he looks outside. And perhaps, just like the wolf, even before realizing that my feet were numb and as stiff as wood from the cold of the night, I thought how hungry I was, that I hadn't eaten for thirty-eight hours, had been maliciously driven from pillar to post, and had covered dozens of kilometers on foot.

Going back to the house, I got up the nerve once again to ask for some bread, saying I'd pay whatever they wanted. They handed me my identity card in silence and I left without thanking them. It was still ten kilometers to Pisa, but I got there, dragging my suitcase behind me. I went through the outlying villages and the city's outskirts almost without noting the horrible destruction, the silence and death reigning in those suburbs where life had once been lively, the workshops full of activity, the houses cheerful and open, the women knitting in doorways. By now I had eaten nothing for almost two days, while walking always amid the ceaseless and hellish rumble of Allied trucks and tanks that sped indifferently by on their way to the front. No one had paid any attention to me, not even the M.P.'s at the checkpoints, and at last I found myself on what had been the river embankment of Pisa.

There I stopped, at a spot where one had once had a view of bridges and the noble panorama of palaces and churches dear to the melancholy Giacomo.* But it looked as though nothing was left. The Arno flowed slowly between two crumbling banks and great reddish blocks of stone; it flowed in the middle of a barren, deserted landscape, full of dust and silence. It was then I understood why people seemed to me so much worse than in the past, now that I had dealt with so many of them in the course of my weary journey. They too had suffered the same fate as the centuries of achievement that represented them; their souls too had caved in like the old city whose every dream had been of wisdom, of age-old experience. Man is always mirrored in the work that represents his history and that of his predecessors, and therein lies the source of his behavior

*The poet Giacomo Leopardi, who in 1827–28 lived for about six months in Pisa; but perhaps also a teasing allusion to "the melancholy Jaques" in Shakespeare's *As You Like It.*—TRANS.

and his reasons for living. Now that mirror had been shattered. Nothing was left but fragments of the most beautiful things: the same was true for him.

I sat on my suitcase thinking these confused thoughts, thinking also, however, that something always remains to man, even when the concrete testimony of his work is lost. He has memory, wisdom, and experience, and when nothing more is left, the images, histories, and spirit of his works remain in his heart, and that spirit cannot easily be overcome. Indeed, it revives more fiercely when nothing else of reality remains to testify to it and make it concrete; it lives more fiercely because it will keep seeking to manifest itself again until it has been rebuilt.

But I was about to drop in my tracks like the previous night. I made an effort, and leaving my suitcase in the debris, I went into a tavern where they gave me a half-liter of wine. I drank it all in one gulp, thinking I'd either be knocked down by it or else it would give me the strength to do the last stretch of road to the center of the city, where I would find something to eat. And that's what happened.

There were still another twenty kilometers separating me from home; this thought dismayed me, but as soon as I felt refreshed, I left the suitcase in a tavern and set out at the same dogged, plodding pace.

It was around the time when one feels the day drawing to a close and is already aware of a sudden nightfall, though the light for a while seems more limpid than ever, that I reached the other side of the mountain made famous by Dante. Once again I saw all the towers of my city, all of them standing, the first city actually left standing after so many ruins. My towers, submerged in a layer of pink light, were there as always, still solid in their elegance; the windows of the city sparkled in the sunset. Around the city walls, amid the hundred churches, amid the polished marbles and gray stones of the patrician palaces, part of the great tragedy had unfolded. Here too there had been death, hatred, horror, foreign oppressors, and foreign liberators, but nothing seemed changed as I approached. It was as though I were falling from a previously unknown height into the placid waters of my childhood.

Sons of Bitches

I had never gone so long without seeing my city. Almost two years had passed, but it seemed much, much longer, two years in which the world's existence had turned centuries upside down, mingling disparate times, races that had never been in contact, hatreds that had never taken a similar form. In physics time has a mathematical aspect of its own, but as experienced and measured by the human mind, it is quite different; its duration, its weight in the human heart have an exclusively metaphysical value, and sometimes a few days are longer than a few centuries. I was seeing my hometown again after an immemorially long period, seeing once more the things it held as though I had abandoned them in another age. Whereas in many years, on returning, I had always found everything the same, found the decrepit life of the place static, petrified perhaps for centuries, after these two years it was now something else.

On the outskirts, seven or eight black soldiers were spreading asphalt on the roadway of the Ozzorri bridge, which had been wrecked by bombs; behind them the superb, elegant towers faded in the last sunlight. This contrast gave me the feeling that fate was pleased to take times, countries, people, and races and mix them up, spilling them out on the earth after rotating them in one of those drums from which the winning lottery number would then be pulled.

My fellow townsfolk, impenitent "hucksters," had bread as always for their untiring teeth. The factories were still for the most part closed, a few had been destroyed, while the war itself had halted a few kilometers away. It had been stagnating on the nearby mountains for several months, one constantly heard the sound of artillery, but my fellow townsfolk went on superbly haggling, with that brisk and infallible deviousness from which I have so deplorably fallen away. Even more than in the past, I felt like a prodigal son without hope of return.

My city was more remote from me than ever, and except for the time spent in the shadow of its polished marbles, illustrious monuments, and innumerable churches, decayed and still alive as in no other part of the world, I whiled away the gray, serene hours alone beside the fireplace, while the shy, fond gaze of my family brooded in silence on the erstwhile child, that child they had never understood, and who, though they didn't know it, no longer existed.

I know the mood of the Italian provinces. I know that life there begins to unfold only at the point where it is able to enclose itself in the heart's secrets, and that human relations are a mute understanding, veiled, forever a mixture of hostility and love, and generous jealousies.

In this sense, Lucca, the Catholic city, the "sacristy of Rome" as some like to call it, has a particular spirit. Social fears, moral reluctance, and everyday contradictions are truly gigantic there, and are forbidden to anyone who does not belong to the solid four-kilometer circle of walls topped with greenery. The churches are rich and crowded, and men and women spend a reasonable portion of their time in them, always ready to beat their breasts over daily "mea culpas." But while the mildness of the gesture is bewildering to those who observe it from outside, not being part of the clan, anyone belonging to that noble world cannot help realizing that at that moment, just when the ritual of individual repentance is unfolding in the shadow of the altars, the keen, intelligent eyes of my fellow townsfolk are rapidly flickering here and there in search of a deal, of the main chance. Beyond this pose, this observance of the law now contained only in gestures, all the rest of society life, albeit under the impenetrable veneer of scrupulous caution left by such practices, is of an unprecedented disorder; there is no moral barrier to stop the progress of anyone trafficking in goods or sometimes in his own honor. Everything is possible, and even where prudence hinders practice and human respect would halt the gesture, the spirit succumbs without hesitation, without regrets. Here is the virgin daughter of a good family who has kept herself physically intact for the man who will have to support her—here she is, her mind overflowing with instinctive carnal knowledge, with every wanton nuance. And here is her mother, who would rather die than yield her daughter's virginity, to which she apparently has sole rights, indirectly prepared to lead her to any moral compromise—only moral ones, of course—whereby she may achieve her purpose and her charms prove diverting and useful to the family, an indirect usefulness as well, but one they both know how to calculate in practical terms. Here, in short, is a world upside down, a world with an insolent veneer of God, and which in its heart boils over with the Devil.

I know my fellow townsfolk and have always found them the same—hard and incapable of change. Each time I've gone back, even after a long absence, it was as though I'd left the day before. But this time, although I had been away for twenty months or so, I felt disoriented; something in them that had held back for centuries had given way in a few weeks. My fellow citizens had loosened up, they had lost part of their hypocrisy, and displayed some of their feelings in their everyday acts. Now there was no need to dig out from behind honeyed appearances things had been hidden for centuries under the black cowl of prudence and social fear. Maybe it was the war, maybe the oppression and the executions, the chance of dying; but what perhaps counted still more were the American boys and their Allied military lire. For the people of Lucca, thousands and thousands of model specimens of four or five Hollywood heroes had arrived, those champions skilled in business, free in love, rich, and ever at the wheels of their cars. Who in those days would have been bold enough to proclaim to my fellow townsfolk that many poor boys from Texas and Oklahoma were humble farmers, truck drivers, workers in toothpaste factories, or garbage collectors? In every one of them they saw an example of American movie life, a standard by which, with only a little hesitation, they might finally discover themselves after centuries of prudence and complaints. I was grateful to the G.I.'s for having worked a miracle, for indeed it was a miracle to have overturned in a few days lives that for thousands of years had kept themselves barricaded and incapable of change. But my fellow townsfolk no longer understood how dangerous it was to remove such a solid, age-old garment without adequate consideration; they did not understand that to "uncover" themselves so suddenly meant laying bare the abominable heap of life's perverse niceties, which had been bundled together, not without elegance and wisdom, over so many centuries of existence and silent mutual regard.

> Tomorrow evening a dance will be held at Palazzo Such-and-such on Via Fillungo. There will also be things to eat and chocolate to drink. All young ladies are invited. Gentlemen cannot be admitted. After the curfew the young ladies will be driven home by car. The last party we had was a great success.

Before this announcement, posted in three of the busiest spots in the city, a little group of men always stopped and pondered the odd syntax. Women didn't stop; it was enough for them to glance at the poster as they went by, read "things to eat," "chocolate," and "driven home by car," and note the day and the address. Certainly plenty of them showed up. For once, bourgeois young ladies presumably did not mind rubbing shoulders with shopgirls and female street vendors, but nevertheless I doubt that the expertly jitterbugging American boys, other than serving chocolate, dancing, and driving the girls home, would have had much else to do. The important thing was that the chocolate and a free supper succeeded in merging social classes that for centuries and centuries had never looked each other in the face. It was not edifying, but I took a malicious joy in it and perhaps I had my reasons.

The British soldiers stationed in our city also held dances, but their poster was quite different. Printed in elegant red and black letters, it set forth the same things in good, almost lapidary Italian, except that at a certain point, so as not to give the appearance of excessive politeness, they had written: "children under 16 and gentlemen not admitted." Here, one must say, was an adroitness that left my poor fellow townsfolk flabbergasted.

I walked through the improvised markets in the city's main squares and mingled with hucksters of all kinds, ripe with age-old experience and the ability to make do. Among them were barbers and blacksmiths who had closed their shops to devote themselves to the new manna of complicated public trading offered by a wartime city behind the lines. But all this saddened me even more and I was unable to relax. I felt a great need for distraction, in order to throw off a kind of steady depression and a great uncertainty that for many months now had almost constantly held me in thrall.

I suspect that people of my age who, like me, wished to gain a particular feeling for the recent past and near future, a sufficient awareness of all the things that had happened at our expense, were not immune to such restlessness. As for myself, it was part of my nature to examine the relation between my inner feelings and whatever I was able to understand of men and things for an answer to guide me, not to knowledge, but in a proper direction close to that justice toward which, however arduously, we ought to be moving.

But my city lends itself poorly to my progress. No sooner am I in it than I'm almost always overwhelmed by the memory and survival of a life now remote but nevertheless important to me. All my youth, its torments, its misfortunes, its attempts to develop according to what at the time seemed to me to be my aspirations; all the memories of sins, of naive loves, of provincial refinements and enthusiasms, seen again in a sharper perspective more conscious of their "effects," keep me from feeling free in my manners and ideas.

This time in Lucca, the weeks went by even more slowly

and restlessly than usual, and at a certain point I felt the need for diversion, but the diversion I sought to organize for myself logically patterned itself on the vestiges of my youthful years: it was basically a reaction to what I had found, an attempt to retrace the stale, fragrant footprints of another time. The places were the same, the people almost the same, and as before I had to invent a lie for my parents.

"I won't be sleeping at home tonight," I said while we were at the dinner table.

"What? Where are you going?"

"To visit friends."

"Who? How? Why?" And it all seemed as childish as before. As in the past, maternal jealousy and paternal suspicion, after some resistance, yielded to the independence I had acquired with such difficulty.

But that night, although everything had been prepared so that the hours would slip pleasantly and cheerfully by, just as supper was almost over a woman started crying. Her problems were no longer the same as before; now she was suffering. Now everyone was suffering much more than before. There had been deaths, there had been unforeseen miseries, quite different from previous ones that in their perseverance had at least had a familiar and lasting ring; they had been the destiny to which one was supposed to resign oneself.

So far we had kept silent, but after these tears we tried to talk. We talked about ourselves, about how when we were younger we were often together as at this moment, but it was though we were talking about the dead. I looked at my female companions while the table was being cleared, and they seemed to me like parodies of the girls I had known before; it was as though they wore masks that distorted their faces, those faces I had come back looking for. Then we thought about going to bed.

"I'll stay here on the couch," I said.

"You want to stay here?" said my companion.

"Yes."

"So goodnight." And she went in another room. We had understood each other completely.

In the morning I fled like a culprit, without saying goodbye. Behind me, a white tombstone was dropped on still another part of my past: rest in peace.

During the final last two weeks I again started wandering around the city, from one street to another, one café to another; then I ran into Mario. We hadn't seen each other for many years and so we had a lot to talk about. Mario is a serious, scornful writer; his writings are full of a resentful lyricism, and he finds it hard to feel at peace with the world. This time, naturally, he was less so than ever; I found him more restless than in the past, full of revolt, the kind of revolt that in all of us now contained a certain hope, however disgruntled it appeared.

Mario is also the head physician at the provincial insane asylum, and he invited me for a tour of inspection. "Come and see our madhouse," he said to me, and the next day I went.

The psychiatric hospital, as it is called on a road sign, stands on a beautiful crest surrounded by open countryside, tilled fields and groves of trees, hills and vineyards. Mario and I had breakfast, we smoked American cigarettes and talked again about our past, then he led me through the gates beyond which we kept hearing moaning and laughter, a singsong that sounded like the tired end of a party taking place in a city of hysterical inhabitants. We entered the women's section. There was a large room where they were working at looms, embroidering, and spinning, and when the new arrival, myself, appeared, many of them gathered around to stare at us in a way I had seen before, though never so full of sincerity. Some of them went on to voice outrageous proposals, addressed to us in a way that stripped us naked in the face of that innocence in which experience and desire have lost all modesty and restraint.

But later the spectacle turned ghastly. In one room thirty women lay on cots in the grip of sinister hallucinations, creatures no longer having anything real about them. "They're starving to death," Mario told me. "In a few weeks they'll all be buried; they're already dead, there's nothing left of them, except a kind of hallucination, the way something of the spirit may perhaps survive when the body is already finished." These women were dying of hunger because during the last period of the war they had had nothing to eat, and now food did them no good; they were dead already. And to convince me of it he uncovered one of them. She looked like one of those rabbit skins that our peasants put out to dry, fur side down, in the sun.

I would just as soon have skipped the rest of it, but before leaving we walked briefly through one of the men's dormitories.

That world, which seems lacking in any sign of humanity, instead has a singularly precise one: every madman is consistent with himself to the bitter end, perfectly consistent with himself. A madman might write the kind of autobiography that has never been written, expressing all his feelings toward his neighbor and himself without ever lying.

One of them lunged at us, yelling, "Sons of bitches!"

His hatred for us was definite, fearless, and unmistakable. I realized that he had endured one of the most painful of human experiences: he felt that the world might consist entirely of enemies, and had decided, come what may, to be the enemy of his fellow man.

"So as not to go crazy you have to be more or less consciously, or more or less deeply, hypocritical," I said to Mario, while trying to come to terms with what I was thinking.

"But if we could only forgive one another, even madness would be overcome," he replied.

Lost Souls

I returned to Rome on a stormy night, curled up in the sleeping compartment of a trailer truck loaded with thousands of brooms.

I was going back to my life, with the feeling that I'd have to face it again as in youth when you first consider the problem of creating a life of your own. I can never think of those days without feeling that these sentiments did not pertain to my particular life, to my difficulties of the moment, but represented something I shared with many others my own age, who had suffered from the sadness not only of the last five years of war, but of the whole period of our youth, locked as it was in an inexorable and falsely decorated armor, even for those who instinctively kept trying to surmount and see beyond it and learn about the world and other things. None of us can forget that it was where we were born, and when we looked around for the first time it seemed like our home, the fatal place imposed on us that allowed for no comparisons, other than by a blind instinct that allowed us to divine what it sought to exclude.

But what, basically, had been my recent experience? Did I already know what one ought to know? These were the kinds of questions I began asking myself, a sign that I was going back to where the children of free peoples are placed at birth. That was perhaps the only way to regain what had been stolen from us in the first half of our existence.

I was born in the shadow of that modest poverty that the more lacking it is in the most elementary worldly necessities, the more it is rewarded and redeemed by loving solidarity, the knowledge of the ties that produce a deep and tormented awareness of life in common.

We, growing up without riches and without true well-being, already had ties as children, a community of interests with the many who shared our fate as poor people. Our fights and games were ties, expressions of the neglected society that protects itself by creating a collectivity, replacing solitary toys with a sense of community that can also be a prelude to the morality of civic life.

But as the years went by, we had the obscure feeling that many things had been denied us. Finally came the war—which is still going on as I write—and with it came for the first time aspects of the world we had never been able to know, even if we had perhaps in part silently reconstructed it intellectually. There came events that managed to awaken deep in our hearts the natural instincts of justice; there came vicissitudes that did not find us completely unprepared; there came the necessity of deciding which side we were on, proving first to ourselves, and then to everyone, that our instinctive and unspecified feelings were related to the most elementary justice. Finally came the time that demanded that we express all this in practice, and then we did not hesitate to take our place beside all those who had risen up.

The twenty-fifth of July[*] had merit for this reason. That it came in 1943 instead of 1939 may have meant something

[*]On 25 July 1943, the king dismissed Mussolini; on 8 September, Marshal Badoglio signed an armistice with the Allies. This was the so-called Forty-five Days, in which Italy went from being an Axis partner to a country occupied by the Germans.—TRANS.

to outsiders who felt called upon to judge us; for us it was simply a day we had been waiting for with increasing awareness and which had finally arrived, still too late and not the way we might have wished.

It was the eighth of September, however, that brought the final resolution, the beginning of a battle. It was on the eighth of September that men and women, even in Rome, were seen weeping in the streets.

Those with whom I had talked until recently about literature, politics, and girls now no longer spoke. Now there was no longer a need for discussion or to evade one's more or less conscious uneasiness by indulging in abstract arguments.

Often it was precisely among those who had seemed to be exclusively taken up with problems thought to be far from reality that I discovered the most resolute individuals prepared for risky operations, while among those who were even ready to fight openly in the streets, it was easier to find an alienated intellectual or an untalkative shopkeeper than some political firebrand. In any case, there were tasks for everyone, and all of them were dangerous.

This was why on the morning of 3 May 1944, a day on which a general strike was supposed to demonstrate—and in some ways did demonstrate—that the people were not submitting to the terror of the enemy, while I was in the company of Fabio, Ennio, and Michele, we found ourselves on a sidewalk where the morning fog was still dense, face to face with four individuals whom it would not have been hard to classify even had they not been pointing guns at our chests.

The sun had not yet succeeded in penetrating to the level of the street, the air was heavy, and not many houses ahead were visible in the fog. Who in those days had not wondered: what will I do if they arrest me? I had often thought about it myself, but I understood in a flash that there was nothing special to be done, and I also had time to realize that for the moment the matter scared me less than I'd imagined.

They took us to a building a short distance from the spot where we had been stopped. I was dragged into a separate room, where I immediately experienced those methods that were already well known and which I now saw I must normally expect pending whatever the outcome was to be.

The tallest of our captors, a man with a cruel face and very white teeth, handcuffed me, pinching my wrists, which at once turned red as the veins swelled around the chain. This first operation completed, he led me to a corner of the room, took my chin and positioned me in such a way that my temple was against an edge of the wall, and began savagely punching me, taking care that with each blow I got a second one from the wall; at the first impact I raised my manacled hands in an instinctive and harmless defensive motion, but this gesture aroused all his fury, and, baring his huge canines, he beat me until I lost consciousness.

I came to a little later in a storeroom no bigger than a closet, which was lined with rifle racks. One of the men was standing nearby; he examined my wrists and, saying, "Does it hurt? Wait a minute," loosened the chain.

Then right away the other one came back with a revolver in his hand, which he pointed at me. He made a rude, unnatural sound with his lips, again displaying his splendid, almost animal-like set of teeth, and yelled, "You'd better tell me everything I want to know, or I'll shoot you on the spot!"

In that moment a host of things went through my mind that might have occupied it for many hours. I was struck by the fact that instead of thinking about what was happening to me, I felt great regret at having to give up, for the time being or even forever, all the things that constituted my usual activities, my daily habits.

Meanwhile, he was screaming like a maniac, beside himself, vulgar and incoherent, "Now you're going to tell me everything."

But I couldn't focus my mind on what he was saying. He started hitting me with the barrel of the revolver, which bounced off my ribs as though it were made of wood.

"I'll kill you!" He sounded desperate. "You'd better tell me who gave you the papers you had in your pocket." Even had I wanted to answer him, I wouldn't have been able to because a feeling stronger than myself was forcing my mind to wander, to remember the obligations I would fail to keep, to think of the work I wouldn't be able to finish. Even today, at this distance of time, what amazes me is the quantity of things that went through my head in those few minutes, although further experience in the weeks to come taught me that this was a wholly instinctive method of self-defense, which in the worst situations allows you to take relatively little notice of the strong-arm tactics of those doing their utmost to make you give in.

After this scene, I was taken back, a little dazed, to the others. We were in a forest rangers' barracks, and they kept us there for a few hours. We were guarded by a nondescript young man who kept his back to the window for fear we would escape. One of the rangers made an effort to talk to us without worrying about compromising himself.

"We're technicians, our business is the woodlands and

always has been." He was indeed a fine mountaineer type. "Now they've made us militiamen, we're part of the *Milizia,* but that's what we've always been, and our job is to take care of the woods and mountains and protect them from disasters." Then he began quietly explaining to me how to avoid landslides, which are one of the great perils of high mountains, then how to fight forest fires, how to reforest places that have become barren, and so on, until a group of city policemen arrived, who after a few formalities took us away in a taxi.

Chained in pairs, we were taken to the Flaminio police station, in whose jail we were held for four days before being sent to other prisons.

The cell in which they put us was indescribably filthy. The floor was of beaten earth, and in the middle was a plank bed of loose boards, on which four or five persons at most could stretch out. The rest either had to stand or lie on the floor.

After I had been there a few hours, along with ten or so individuals of every sort, I realized at last that I had crossed the threshold of my usual life. Already I felt detached from everything that had concerned me until a few hours before, and I quickly formed a new psychology that allowed me to lose all interest in everything that was happening to me.

A haggard-looking man with a black mustache and a short little jacket, his patent-leather shoes coming to a thin point, stationed himself in the middle of the central wall and started talking to everyone without anyone asking him.

"They say I stole a wallet. Is it my fault if it was lying right there at my feet?"

"Where?"

"On the tram. They started yelling, then they put the blame on me."

He fell silent. I was thinking he must really have stolen it, and the silence of the others expressed the same idea.

"And you, why are you here?" I asked a miserable sort of man with a sweet, lost look on his face; he was sitting, arms dangling, on the far corner of the plank bed. His flesh could be seen through the holes in his ragged garments, and just looking at him induced a great sadness. He answered, clucking his tongue in an effort to express himself; his words sounded like a mixture of several dialects, and it was with some difficulty that we learned he'd been arrested for tearing down a wall poster.

"Why did you tear it down?"

"I just did, that's all."

"What did it say?"

"There was . . . I mean . . . it showed a soldier. I was waiting for my . . . my brother-in-law at the street corner."

"But why did you tear it down?"

"Heh, heh, heeeh." He laughed without answering, his flabby, wet mouth half covered by his long beard.

Very many of those put into that cell during the day were individuals picked up here and there for no reason, and destined to dig trenches on the Anzio front. A German truck came at around eleven o'clock every night to take them away.

Never in my life had I seen such a filthy place, a room a few meters square where at a certain point as many as twenty-five men were locked up, which meant that most of them had to remain standing.

In the four days I was kept there, before beginning the circuit of other cells in jails old and new, about a hundred prisoners passed through, most of them between twenty-five and thirty-five years old. Desperate, resigned faces, sometimes clean and with pomaded hair, more often unkempt and dirty, worn by privation. Those with the most miserable appearance were gloomy but never complained; the rare well-dressed ones stood in the corners moaning that they wanted to telephone home. Petty thieves, however, protested in loud voices, cursed and blasphemed. My particular memory of those four days is the rapid succession of all these characters, each of them an experience for me, an image whose meaning increasingly departed from anonymity to represent something I've never understood well, but which seems to me to be summed up by the thought that their common fate—leaving aside the few street thieves—gave them a common face, a feeling that increasingly stood out in them all, solidly beneath their elementary differences. Through this succession of characters, I felt I was witnessing on a small scale the unifying process that was becoming more concrete the more the effects of oppression became apparent in our daily life.

A police sergeant brought in two individuals who spat and talked nonstop between themselves. "Not your lucky day!" he said in a loud voice. "There were twenty-five thousand lire in that wallet."

They kept talking to each other without interruption until evening, when, turning to the rest of us, they said, "We've both got T.B. and we mean to sleep on the boards."

Ennio and I, cowed by this kind of psychological terrorism, which made us even more aware of the dirt and dampness of the place, spread a blanket on the ground, and slept beneath the circling feet of those on the plank bed and those unable to find a place.

I wouldn't be able to say why I will always remember three young fellows who made a considerable impression on me during the ten or twelve hours they were held. They had been arrested while bringing from the countryside a few head of cattle destined for the black market. They came from far away; they were tired and baked by the sun, having driven the animals, which they had bought from peasants, across hills and woodlands. I was attracted by their speech, its rebellious tone; each of their gestures was like a gesture of revolt. They wore rough clothes like peasants, and the more I looked at them the more absolutely elegant they appeared.

"We bought the animals in Anguillara and we've been walking for two days," said one, as he shared some country bread with us and lean ham cut in long, thick slices. "They'd better let us go soon, otherwise the animals won't get fed."

"We want to work," added a second with conviction.

"We've always worked, we work when we can and we earn a lot, but we can never stop." Thus remarked the third, who lay stretched out the whole time, gazing at the ceiling. They talked as though someone were contradicting them.

"This is no life, but we want to live all the same—anyway, there'll be other times." They were resentful, calm, secure; they emphasized their words with rapid gestures of the hand. They spoke of the war, of their work, and looked around them, troubled, with the large, serene eyes of the Roman people.

"We've been fighting a war! Nothing but war. Even our work is a constant war."

The one who was always lying down then concluded without moving, "The wars will end. There's been nothing but wars, that's true. But they'll end before we do!"

The three of them were together because they were alike, strong and handsome, troubled and polite. One of their angry gestures said more to me than all their words. The Sicilian watched wide-eyed, his mouth half open; every so often he tried to speak, but the words died on his lips. They laughed and asked him, "Why did you tear down the poster?"

"'Cause, 'cause, because—" Then he too laughed, unable to go on. Later, while everyone was silent, we heard a kind of slow whimpering that little by little became a subdued weeping, sad as that of an inconsolable child. We turned around, and it was the Sicilian who was weeping; that ragged, bearded man had collapsed in a corner with his head between his knees and was crying his heart out. If he hadn't been so dirty, one of us would have gone over and stroked his bristly head.

"What are you crying about, you jerk!"

Later the three cattle drovers went away, and as they left they gave me a crushing handshake.

Toward evening on the third day, at the most depressing hour, the hour when almost all of a sudden it turned dark and the air became more unbreathable than ever, at the moment in which for a short while each retreated into his own silence to ponder resignation, preparing his indifference to everything that might happen, they came to take me and my three friends. We were awaiting this call, we had talked about it, and each had prepared something to say that would match what the others said.

They led us handcuffed to the floor above, where some police inspector or other was waiting for us: up the stairs we went, chained two by two; then, starting with the youngest, we were each called into the presence of our inquisitor. As far as I was concerned, much as I had tried, I had settled on nothing specific in advance. I knew that on this first interrogation many things would depend for me and the others, but I'd been unable to formulate a plan and hadn't insisted further, thinking it might perhaps be easier for me to behave according to what the situation would require of me at the moment.

Once I was in the presence of this man, though he threw out his chest and carefully looked me over with his dull, gray eyes, I felt secure enough. I sat down, then got up again because the glare of the last sunlight from the window was in my eyes; not that it bothered me, but I had the feeling of thereby adopting a confident attitude, and perhaps I wasn't entirely wrong, because right after this gesture, my interlocutor looked somewhat uncertain. He was a young man but with completely white hair; there was a certain elegance about him, but also something vulgar, if not in his features, in his slight movements and in his posture at the desk in front of which I was seated on a straw-bottomed chair. There was a moment of silence; he looked at me, and I made an effort to stare back at him with a calm that actually was not feigned.

"I know all about you," he began. "I know very well who you are. I know you'll try to win me over by playing the wiseguy, the witty man of the world." I figured I owed this opening to my nonchalant gesture of a few minutes before and didn't answer.

"I'm a Fascist and you're not, which means we're enemies." He said this in an almost solemn tone. Then he explained that he respected clear-cut positions, and from his rather muddled discourse I had the impression he wanted to give a diplomatic tone to our conversation. I spread

The World Is a Prison

my arms without answering, as though to state that I had no objections.

"Your life absolutely depends on what you say."

"I know." Already in those three days, I had been told more than once that I might be shot.

"We haven't yet been to your house," he went on. This remark suggested to me the opposite, making me decide on the spur of the moment to say, without seeming to, much more than he may have wanted, to state with indifference what they would find in searching my apartment, since I was now sure they had already turned it upside down. In the course of these declarations, I saw he was listening nervously; he was expecting me to conceal anything that might have compromised me, thus allowing him at the end to catch me in contradiction by telling me what he already had in his hands. While I went on explaining, as though I didn't care, he bit his lip.

Carried away finally by my own words, I invented a fictitious character, gave him the name Giovanni, and stated that I had met him in places that actually I hardly knew. When the stenographer fell behind, I repeated what I had said.

Toward the end, the voice of Fancy Pants became shriller and more threatening, but now the fact of having talked so much had given me a calmness I would not have suspected in myself. Since we were making no progress, he decided to tell me: "Well, we've been to your house."

"Okay, I told you myself what was there," I replied.

He got up without further ado. He had obviously counted on putting this last revelation to a different use and was quite irritated about it.

"We'll meet again soon!" He strode rapidly out of the room, clearly annoyed with himself.

We were back in our prison cell, crowded in with twenty other unfortunates, and I was feeling pleased with myself, perhaps like a schoolboy who has done well on an exam, when I was recalled. This second summons came unexpectedly and made me nervous, since I had no idea what it meant.

I was taken to the office of the police chief, who was waiting for me together with another gentleman wearing a blood donor's lapel pin; they looked at me and smiled, asked me to sit down, and after a moment of silence: "What party do you belong to?"

I hemmed and hawed, without saying anything definite.

"Catholic Communists, right?"

After a brief pause, reassured by their conciliatory air, beginning to understand, though still suspicious, but convinced it was what they wanted to hear, I replied, "Yes."

Whereupon the police chief and the blood donor got up, shook hands with me without speaking, and I was taken back to the cell.

A few hours later the grille in the cell door was opened, and the beaming face of the blood donor appeared between the bars. I saw he was looking for me and approached; he touched my hand, smiled, and said in a low voice: "Don't worry, your interrogation went fine. Don't worry, don't worry." And off he went, reassuring me with mysterious gestures of promise.

I didn't know what it was all about, but I felt pleased as I went back to the others—we had friends out there.

The next morning there was a lot of commotion. Many people had been rounded up, including a couple of petty thieves. There were volleys of groans and curses, but many kept silent, crouching in the corners and thinking about their own cases, or indifferent to what was going to happen to them. Some, however, wanted to talk, but it was hard for them to find someone ready to listen for more than a few minutes: if you went on too long, you realized that the listener was staring at a point on the wall, thinking about his own situation; at a certain moment, he would turn toward the speaker amazed that he was still talking about something.

A young blond fellow dressed in blue kept coming over to me; he would look at me, start to say something, but I was one of those with little desire to listen. Perhaps amid that crowd, within the few square meters of those four filthy walls, he thought he saw in me someone who might even listen to him.

After hours and hours of trying, while I was looking the other way, he said to me without warning: "In our family we do what comes to mind. Whatever goes through our heads. Even my dad."

"Nothing wrong with doing what goes through your head," I said inadvertently.

"Yeah, a week ago I was still working. Now I'm unemployed."

"Tonight at eleven," I replied, since I was now familiar with the routine, "they'll hand you over to the Germans, who'll give you all the work you want. They'll take you to Anzio."

"And not you?"

"No, I suspect I'm bound for someplace else."

"You know, I was working for the Germans just a week ago. I had a job at Fono Film. I do photography. But I left the place." He paused, then, since I didn't ask, he went on: "I'd finished developing a roll of film, I was bending down to unstop the drain on the floor, which had got clogged and made the water back up in the pipe, but while I was in that position I started thinking: what am I doing this for? So I got up and took a cane that was standing in a corner, I got furious and broke everything, trays, light fixtures, cameras; I smashed the whole room, then I went out in the courtyard and kicked over two big earthenware pots with two little myrtle plants growing in them, the pots were fastened with wire but I knocked them over just the same and they broke. The Germans could see what was going on: they were watching me from a distance. I thought I'd really get it in the neck, but instead after a while they sent for me, paid me what was owing me, and sent me away. Bye-bye!"

"And what came into your mind?"

"What am I doing this for? That's what came into my mind."

I looked at him and shook my head; he went on: "Things just happen . . . like that! Can you guess what I did this morning?" he continued without a pause. "I got up early, went to church, and took communion . . . Yes, communion!" I nodded.

"Then I took the tram. I wanted to go and buy some flowers to put in front of the Madonna in the courtyard of my house. When I got to the first stop, I stuck my head out the window and looked at the flower sellers' stands. They were ugly, the flowers they had, so I said to myself: that woman who sells flowers at the next stop will have better ones, I'll go that far, and I kept going. In fact, I got off at the next stop, and two cops grabbed me, almost picked me up bodily, and brought me here. But I protested."

"If you'd got off at the first stop, they wouldn't have grabbed you."

"Sure, if I'd got off back there. But they won't keep me long. Anyway, I don't care."

"You won't enjoy digging trenches for their war."

"I was a soldier till the eighth of September."

"But isn't it different now?"

"I can't figure it out."

"But we ought to try to figure it out a little, otherwise . . ."

"Every day now I think something different, depending on what comes into my head . . ."

Outside we heard the rumble of a truck.

"Here they are," I said. "It's your turn now."

Indeed, as happened every evening, those who had been rounded up during the day were led outside, and the rumble of the truck faded in the night. A few of us were left behind in silence. It was the third time I had witnessed this departure, and the third day that I and my three friends had been locked up here without knowing what they meant to do with us.

"At least they're getting some fresh air," someone said. And we settled down to sleep on the dirt floor.

At dawn we were still stretched out on the floor, until it was broad daylight and the first new detainees began arriving. For four days now we hadn't taken off our shoes, and our hands were black with dirt.

The police chief and the blood donor had me brought upstairs once again. They declared themselves even more openly and made promises to me.

At eight in the morning a boy had been brought in who crouched in silence in a corner and slept, peaceful and indifferent; he was followed by the usual fifteen or twenty unfortunates whose guilt consisted in having taken one street instead of another. Around ten they brought in a young man of twenty, clean-shaven and wearing a light-colored suit. He was no sooner inside than he started almost running the width of the cell, striking his forehead over and over in desperation. He was so desperate that at a certain point I tried to console him.

"Don't give up hope. I'd gladly change places with you. They've been holding me here for four days and I don't know what they mean to do with me. Instead, this evening you'll be in the open air, and then somehow or other, don't worry, you'll land on your feet." He looked at me without replying, and continued running back and forth.

"Don't let it upset you."

"If only it were that easy, but I know . . . I know . . ." Then he stopped, frightened. He was afraid to speak. But during the day he calmed down.

"Why do you get so upset?" I asked, more to get him to talk than to comfort him.

"That's easy to say. If you only knew . . ."

"Knew what?"

"Nothing, don't make me talk. I don't want to talk!"

"With me you can talk."

"Don't make me talk, you want to destroy me?" And for another hour he kept silent, while I, my curiosity aroused, tried every so often to get something out of him. He kept resisting, but slowly yielded.

"If you only knew where I'm coming from, where I was only five days ago, and now here I am again." Then, as though recovering himself: "No! No, don't make me talk, I don't want to go back there!" Saying this, his features contracted.

"Don't tell me anything if you don't want to."

"That's not the point. I promised never to say anything.

I got out of there swearing I wouldn't say a word about what I'd seen . . ."

"Where?"

"I can't talk. I tell you I can't."

Then he started asking me why I was here, why they had held me for four days in this place where ordinarily they didn't keep anyone for more than a day and a night. I explained to him why my friends and I were here. He hesitated, then said: "Five days ago I left Via Tasso. I spent ninety days there, and now I'm here again!" And saying this, he struck his forehead with his hands, looking around to be sure no one else was listening.

By now the prisons on Via Tasso had become famous. From the moment I'd been arrested I was thinking that was where I'd end up. So more than ever I tried to get this fellow to speak, but whenever he started talking, he would stop in fear.

"What's Via Tasso like? Are the cells like this one? Are they worse than this?" He stared at me, made a gesture with his hands as though he considered me hopelessly naive but didn't want to say more.

"I suspect that's where I'll end up," I said.

"Probably," he replied. "If it happens, remember to let go, don't make a fuss about anything; you'd better realize you're no longer a man. That's my advice to you. If you have any cigarettes, hide them in the sleeves between your shirt and jacket, that's the only place they don't think to look." Again he retreated into silence and there was no more possibility of getting him to talk. No sooner would he start to say something than he stopped, terrified.

"I can't, I can't talk about it."

And when I insisted, he said: "You want me to end up

there again? You want to destroy me? Please drop the subject." Toward evening a blond man in a turtleneck jersey began talking about a naval battle and a shipwreck. While everyone was silently following his words, or perhaps thinking about their own situations while letting themselves be soothed by his voice, which was like a lullaby, and I stared at the ceiling with my hands under my head, I was called along with Ennio and Fabio. Michele had been released a few hours earlier.

An Amateurish Setup

Waiting for us outside stood a shiny automobile with four men, who without speaking made us get in. After a long and aimless ride, we drove toward the Prati quarter and finally entered the grim gateway of the Mussolini Barracks. The car stopped in the middle of the courtyard, where about a hundred young boys were standing with bayonets at the ready.

The kids with the bayonets formed a large circle around the car, staring at us from a distance as though they were afraid of us. The minutes passed and there we sat, while the circle of armed boys slowly narrowed; they approached with short steps as though intent on storming a redoubt. As they came closer and I was able to look many of them right in the face, I recalled an item that had appeared in the underground newspapers, which said that a high percentage of the militias had been recruited in juvenile reformatories. But the circle kept narrowing and no one came to get us; now some were a few steps away—they brandished their fists but with a curious hesitation, as though we inspired in them a certain fear. Another few minutes went by; they were now at the doors of the car; they stuck their fists through the windows, and some pointed their bayonets at us. I looked at the faces of my two companions, who were holding their breath. But now a platoon of seven or eight of them arrived with fixed bayonets; they halted, placed themselves on either side of us, and escorted us into the barracks prison.

It was a large, clean room, with a huge window and a sloping plank bed capable of holding at least fifteen people.

As one entered, the only object in the whole place that stood out, as though it had been put there on purpose, was a mess tin with a spoon lying crosswise on top of it. Then there were two individuals, a fat, well-dressed gentleman and a little man with a long beard. The room looked more like a set for a propaganda film than a real prison. We were hardly inside when the fat man, gazing at me as I contemplated the spoon and mess tin, which was half full of rice, remarked almost absentmindedly, "There's nothing to eat at this hour, he was eating when they came to get him."

"Who?"

"The guy who was with us, the one who was eating from that mess tin." I said nothing, but I was already forming an opinion of these two new cellmates. "They took him to Forte Boccea," the fat man went on. "They've shot him by this time, that's for sure. His house was full of weapons." I looked at Ennio and Fabio, and it seemed to me they were thinking the same thing.

"I'm a lawyer," continued the fat man. "They've got me here because I'm accused of having a list of people who were supposed to be killed."

Still I said nothing. There was a short silence, then the other one, turning to Fabio, who was Jewish, began: "You look familiar. Haven't I seen you in Via del Pianto, at the Portici d'Ottavia, near Piazza Campitelli?"

"I doubt it," said Fabio. "That's nowhere near where I live."

"My mistake then," said the little man. Then, after a

pause: "And yet I'd swear I know you, that I've seen you in that neighborhood."

"I doubt it. I never go there."

"My mistake, but you do look familiar." Fabio said nothing more. I picked up a blanket.

"You've taken his," said the fat man.

"Whose?"

"The guy they just shot at Forte Boccea. He always covered himself with that blanket." I spread it on the plank bed and lay down.

"You've picked the same place. That's where he always slept."

There were a few moments of silence. The three of us were sitting on the wooden planks and the other two were standing apart and chatting. After a while the fat man came over to me, affable and smiling.

"Don't be upset," he said. "It's no fun being here, but what can we do?"

"Nothing," I replied.

"What did you fellows do to end up here? These people aren't kidding, you know!"

Then a guy with a lot of daggers came in to bring us coffee. He spoke with a Florentine accent and had a slimy look; jangling a bunch of keys, he served us with affected courtesy. "I can't help it," he said. "It's my thankless job to be a jailer here."

"To each his own."

"Yeah, that's true," he replied. "Coffee tomorrow morning, and later on meat and risotto—that okay with you?" he concluded with a timid smirk of irony as he went away.

It was starting to get dark. We settled down for the night, thinking almost with relief of the four other nights we had just spent in the police station on Via Flaminia. As we lay there in silence, the fat man came over and started talking to me.

"They'll interrogate you tomorrow morning. There's a special room here in the barracks—really, it's not pleasant. They tie you up in special chairs, or on specially made cots, and then they've got a thousand ways to make you talk whether you want to or not."

Even without discussing it, we had understood perfectly what sort of cellmates we had, and we tried to appear more indifferent than was possible. The man went on explaining tortures, with the most affable of smiles and the most malicious of placid expressions on his face.

As I stretched out to try to get some sleep, he said, "You've picked the same place as he. That's just where he used to sleep until last night."

Then he took a blanket and lay down near me. His tone became fatherly, affectionate: "You must be about the same age as my son. I'm a lawyer, you can ask my advice if you like. I've been in this cell myself for several days and who knows what they mean to do with me."

"Thanks, I really don't have . . . I wouldn't know what . . ."

"I could be your father," he said to me again, then began talking about politics, recent events, the war. Sleepy as I was, I too started talking, saying the strangest, most innocuous things. I went on and on with no letup, and the more I spoke, the more I felt a kind of euphoric pleasure in saying whatever passed through my head, for the relish of seeing that individual intently listening to all my arguments in the hope of catching something of interest to him. I can't remember everything I said, but I talked about women, about religion, literature, and didn't stop until I saw that my listener, his head drooping slowly on his chest, was no longer following me. For some reason or other, I even said I'd like to have two children. He perked up slightly, gave me an astonished look, then fell asleep snoring. After a while I too fell asleep, and woke up only when a vulgar song, familiar since boyhood, drifted in from the courtyard. It was the beardless soldiers singing the imperial anthems, the old marching songs of the Fascist death squads.

Until ten o'clock we saw no one; then they came to call us. I thought they were taking us upstairs for interrogation, but instead another deluxe automobile was waiting for us, in which we were seated amid the usual poker faces. So was it another unknown destination? The car drove toward Piazza Colonna, where the new leadership of the Fascist party had its headquarters.

There they made Ennio get out. After sitting in the parked car for twenty minutes, Fabio and I were again driven through the center of the city in the direction of Santa Maria Maggiore. The two of us exchanged a wordless look: we had understood.

Prison without Light

Via Tasso was blocked by two rows of chevaux-de-frise guarded by two policemen; on the other side of the barricade were empty crates, barbed wire, and automobiles parked in front of the prison.

We were led inside, along several corridors, to the door of an office; while we waited, SS officers passed back and forth, all armed with riding crops. They glanced at us and went on their way.

Once we were inside, our names were listed, then we were taken to a room where, one at a time, we were searched and stripped of everything. While they were searching Fabio, I was made to stand with my face to the wall, and when I leaned against it with one shoulder, a noncommissioned officer noticed and shoved me back in the previous position, indicating with a gesture that I'd be in trouble if I did it again. Thus I learned the first rule of Via Tasso. When they took Fabio away, he started to put out his hand to me as he passed, only to be stopped by a sharp blow on the shoulder.

When all these procedures were over, I was taken again along the hallways of all those offices, then through a small doorway that was opened by ringing a bell: I found myself at the foot of a stairway. A German spoke on a telephone, then motioned to me to go upstairs. It was the staircase of a modern apartment building whose rooms had been turned into prison cells, an ordinary staircase, clean and paved with green marble. One's first feeling on the way up, despite the familiar look of the place, was consternation instead of reassurance. It was like climbing the stairs to some rented apartment where a friend lives who often invites you to dinner—but on the first landing there was a soldier with a club in his hand and a big revolver on his hip. He motioned to me to keep going, and so one floor after another I arrived at the fifth, where another soldier with huge shoulders was waiting for me, keys in hand. He took me through what had been the door of one of the fifth-floor apartments, and I found myself in a short hallway lit by an electric bulb. I don't know why, but it gave me the impression of an industrial installation: I felt as though I were facing the compartments of a refrigerating plant or something. It wasn't easy to get an idea of it, but it didn't suggest a prison. There was a stale, tepid smell, like the typical odor of sheds where they keep a lot of rabbit hutches. One suddenly felt that the air was bad, and that invisible beings had been brought together and locked up here as in so many closets. I was taken through a doorway that bore the number 31, and for a moment it was so dark I could see nothing. I stopped for a few seconds, until I saw something moving in the background: there were white faces, the pallor of some set off by the darkness of long, black beards. Then I saw a tall, thin body, transparent as a ghost.

There were already four people there: we looked at each other for a moment, then I sat down on the floor in a corner. I was tired. Someone extended his hand.

"I'm Piero."

Another: "I'm Carlo." Then Pasqualino and Luciano.

Meanwhile, I was starting to get used to the darkness. I

realized all of a sudden that they were sitting around me in a circle and waiting.

"I'm Guglielmo," I said.

They gathered closer around me, asking two at a time, "Where do you come from? How is the war going?" I didn't know where to begin. I was tired and hesitated a moment, whereupon Piero cried to the others, "But let him breathe! Let him rest!"

Carlo stared at me without speaking; the others also kept silent as I looked around. The cell, which must have been three meters long and slightly more than one and a half in width, was faintly lit by artificial light coming in from the small grating over the door. Even sitting down like this, we took up almost all the space and it was hard to breathe.

"I've been here in the dark for sixty days now," said Piero, getting to his feet with difficulty. The others had also been there for a long time and their faces were white as alabaster. Only Carlo still had a little color and the firmness of his broad northerner's face; the faces of the others were transparent, long and oval, on which a common expression created a surprising resemblance.

We had been silent for a while, when I heard a voice that seemed to come from an underground distance: "31, 31!"

Luciano answered: "What do you want, 28?"

"Did they bring someone new?"

"Yes."

Another voice, still farther away: "Who is it?"

"He still hasn't told us, he's tired." Then we heard the heavy tramp of a jailer and there was a silence that seemed boundless.

"Who was that talking?" I asked.

The World Is a Prison

"Quiet," they said in a low voice, and Pasqualino added, "Don't forget to jump to your feet whenever you hear the door open." The German's footsteps receded.

"After we eat we'll have to check you out," said Carlo, laughing. I had no idea what he meant, but I smiled and didn't ask.

Then little by little, with increasingly rapid-fire questions, they kept me talking for a long time. They wanted to know what the Germans were doing in the city, what people were saying about the war, what they thought of the Anzio landing, at what time was the curfew, if once in a while there was still firing in the streets, the price of eggs and the color of rationed bread. After an hour Luciano called out to cell 28 and in an allusive and often incomprehensible language repeated everything I had been able to tell them. Many voices, which sounded distant and buried, could be heard commenting—a few pessimistic remarks, a few joking observations, then it seemed to me they all fell silent, waiting for something.

"We'll eat shortly," someone explained to me. And soon we heard a receptacle being set down on the landing: immediately there was the sound of cell doors being opened one by one, and my companions started counting.

"Now they're at 28, now 29, 30; now it's our turn, line up and do like us . . ."

We each got a bowl of some abominable swill and two round loaves. They sniffed the bread and I sniffed it too: it stank. I put it all down on a blanket with disgust; they gave me furtive looks.

"You don't like it."

"You sure don't like it."

"Don't worry, you'll like it in a few days," said Carlo. "Right now you still have a little fat in your stomach, but once you've used it all up you'll eat anything."

"Since you're new, today you get to be next to last."

"For what?"

"To choose the bread."

"Go ahead and choose, they're all the same, aren't they?"

"If you look closely, they're not all the same. So pay attention, here's what we do: we put all ten loaves together, whoever is last gets to divide them up into groups of two, then the first guy takes his pick, then the second, and so on. Today you're next to last, tomorrow you'll be last, and the day after tomorrow first."

It seemed to me they were overdoing it, but I didn't say anything. I sat watching their maneuvers. The last one for that day, squatting on the floor, measuring and calculating in a hairsplitting way, took at least ten minutes to divide up the five portions. Then each in turn took his portion after lengthy consideration, having first circled around and weighed each pair of loaves in his hands. I still didn't see the point; it seemed to me these maneuvers were a kind of diversion to pass the time, but their diligence was truly impressive.

"You can have my soup," I said, and they looked at me in disbelief. Some protested feebly, but already they were all simultaneously reaching out for my bowl. Again there was a lengthy and meticulous division, while I chewed my bread, which had an odd taste of kerosene.

"You won't get anything more to eat until this time tomorrow," Pasqualino told me. I was struck by his words, and for the first time began to see our situation in its true light.

Meanwhile, I was having trouble breathing. I said so, and they told me that during the first days it was always like that.

"There's no air here, but you get used to it. Don't ever stand up suddenly because it'll make you dizzy." And indeed, every time I got up, I had to lean against the wall and put my hand to my forehead.

Having finished the bread, I stretched out on the floor. The others did likewise, and there was an hour of silence. Piero, in breathing, every so often wheezed and groaned. When I turned toward him, he smiled.

At first, a hand under my neck, submerged in the darkness of the cell, I listened. Every so often one heard a guard's heavy tread; sometimes a sigh that seemed to come from underground, a fit of coughing, the dragging of a foot made me ever more aware that all around me, within the restricted space of a few meters, other beings like ourselves, invisible and benumbed, felt themselves above all prisoners of the inexorable slowness of time, of the continual drone of hours, days, and nights. But in the first days the mind often reached out, and in a few moments it was possible to relive the greater part of one's life, to rediscover faces we might never have remembered, landscapes full of silence. With the passage of time, however, a kind of languor grew inside the body, a subtle torment that made your arms fall like death and your chin droop on your chest. Often it was hard to realize what was the matter, but at a certain point it came like a flash: hunger. And that was the borderline where despair was born; after a violent upsurge of this sudden sensation, you spent the day without seeing, without saying a word. In the evening, however, someone would yell: "No, I can't stand it anymore."

"Shut up," said the others. "You want to drive us all

crazy? Say something! Somebody tell us a story." And someone would start talking.

But it took me several days to learn all this. At that moment I lay with my arms under my neck, immersed in the darkness of the cell, and with a certain buzzing in my ears, a certain torpor in my limbs, and this was not unpleasant. It reminded me of the sluggish indolence of adolescence.

"It looks like we haven't decided anything for this evening," said Carlo an hour later.

"Yeah, we still haven't thought about it, but now that Guglielmo's here we ought to cook up something new," replied Pasqualino, serious and concerned, looking at me as I lay on the floor. I still didn't understand, and let them go on.

"I'll do the menu," said Carlo. "We could have them fix us some chilled consommé."

"You know I don't like consommé," Luciano put in.

"Don't interrupt, you don't have to drink it. Chilled consommé and a slice of ham with butter." I raised my head, looking at the faces of my new companions, but they had gathered in a circle, arguing with a kind of doggedness, and scarcely looked back at me.

"Then veal cutlets with marsala. You like cutlets with marsala?"

I was disconcerted by their seriousness and answered yes by nodding my head.

"Veal cutlets with marsala and a salad of white lettuce on the side, red wine, then we'll send out for ice cream from the bar on the corner."

"No, no ice cream. Coffee and a brandy."

"I'm all for ice cream . . ." At this point a long discussion ensued, and I, who from the beginning had listened smiling, all of a sudden felt terribly dismayed. I had the feeling they believed everything they were saying, and watched them argue as to whether ice cream after supper was a good idea or not. There was something in all this that I found distasteful, and without meaning to I suddenly stood up, bracing myself against the wall. Then they all turned and looked at me gravely, and Piero cried, "Hey, we forgot to check him out!"

I saw them jump on me as though they were ready to lynch me. Piero and Carlo stuck their hands in both pockets of my pants, the other two in those of the jacket. Then they removed their hands, spread a towel underneath me, and started over, carefully turning out all the pockets, including the lesser ones. From the inside pocket of the jacket fell a cigarette butt, and Pasqualino exclaimed triumphantly, "This guy's a capitalist!"

Along with lint, a few almost imperceptible bits of tobacco had fallen on the towel, such as might be found in the creases of any man's pockets. Patiently they collected them, without bothering to separate them from the lint, for otherwise there wouldn't have been much left. Then they shredded the cigarette butt and all of them, happy, kneeling on the floor, gave me a thankful look.

"We'll smoke this as soon as we get a light."

"You Never Talk about Anything"

So far I hadn't given it much thought, but I soon realized
that in Via Tasso one was tragically a prisoner not only of
abstract time, submerged in a slow and droning darkness,
not only of the pangs of hunger, but also of the Germans.

Then I experienced a new kind of suffering. I had found
calm, at times an endless lazy and unconscious serenity in
silence, but it was not like that for the four others. Silence
was their greatest enemy, capable of making them mean
and violent, of streaking their faces with tears, until they
burst out in curses, in cries of terror and impotent revolt.
That was why they talked, why they rose up in protest when
a devious and powerful silence descended on the cell. "Why
doesn't someone say something!" they would yell, and
someone would start talking. Their voices often grew
depressed and monotonous; sometimes their speech
turned complicated, abstract; it became a monologue, endless and senseless, but the words flowed like a constant
trickle of water. They talked, and as for myself, I had very
little to say; indeed, I realized that when I did say something, I had the same feeling as though I were writing a
page. I was unable to construct images for them, only arguments that at times made them nervous, at times attentive
and disconcerted. When they talked, every word was an
image, every discourse a teeming world of characters, emotions, children, mothers, and lovers.

"You never talk," one or another of them often said to

me, and I suffered from this a little. "You never talk" didn't mean I kept silent, but rather that I never had anything to talk about, and it was true, so true that it made me feel humiliated, especially when one of them, for the principle of the thing, because he felt the absolute need for it, began to talk, the way an open faucet discharges an endless flow of water, monotonous but pleasant to listen to, and capable of distracting those oppressed by something.

There was absolute silence, however, when Luciano prayed. He prayed for half an hour in the morning and for half an hour after our sad meal. The first day I didn't understand: I saw him get up and stand against the wall, looking straight ahead, with his hands on his chest, but I didn't realize they were clasped. The others would fall silent as soon as he got up, and they all turned away from him, overcome by a slight embarrassment and by a deep respect for this boy, who was staring at an almost invisible little medal stuck somehow on the wall and for thirty minutes was no longer aware of us. Every so often he raised his eyes as though the sky were above him, but there was only the low ceiling and the everlasting darkness, at least when the light wasn't on. For each cell had a large bulb that sometimes lit up, illuminating the small room so abruptly that each of us put his hand over his eyes, which momentarily felt painful and clouded. Luciano prayed and there was silence; some put their heads in their hands, and maybe they were praying too. These were the moments most readily followed by an anxiety that gradually took hold of everyone; then each huddled in his corner, his portion of darkness, and all that could be heard was our mutual breathing.

For me such moments represented a kind of almost perfect placidity. As usual, these solitary individuals in such a small space, each lost in a world intangible to the others, by the expression of their sadness incited me to the opposite, and I became all of a sudden placid and indifferent. Thus I looked at their faces, followed their now unseeing eyes, and I had the feeling of running after their thoughts, which tended of course toward the family—simple thoughts based entirely on homely images.

Pasqualino was my age. He was very composed, quite short, but his stature, like that of all true citizens of Rome, was compensated by the rough-hewn, well-proportioned harmony of his limbs. His face was oval-shaped, with small and sharp eyes. He had had many jobs, but there was one that he loved and still remembered with almost burning nostalgia: he had enjoyed being a butcher, perhaps because the memories of his life as a butcher were mingled with the brightest memories of his early youth, his lucky times as a poor and happy boy.

"In the morning all the servant girls in the quarter would come to our shop," Pasqualino always said when, in the heavy silence, a sob or curse threatened to explode in someone with a gesture of despair that would drive the others further into a boundless sadness. "All the servant girls came by and, believe me, when Pasqualino was there, they had a ball. Not many butchers knew how to cut up an animal like I did, detach the shoulder and carve big, even cuts of lean meat, and while I kept carving away I'd talk to the girls and they all came over to my side of the shop. The boss and his wife saw what was going on, and in fact when I got married the boss's wife called me over and said, 'Listen, Pasqualino, now that you're getting married, we're going to raise your wages, but you mustn't tell the customers, you understand, because the girls go for bachelors. You won't tell them, will you?' 'Of course not,' I said, and from that day on I started having a lot of fun, because anytime I paid a compliment to some servant girl, I'd look over at the boss's wife sitting behind the cash register and she'd give me a wink and we'd have a good laugh, without the girls knowing what it was all about."

Then Pasqualino, his hands under his head, would close his eyes and smile, completely contented. There was something in his life, which he could go on talking about for three or four hours at a stretch, that I felt I understood perfectly and which at the same time was remote from me and inaccessible. There was something in it that resembled happiness, a happiness like many others destroyed by the war, for Pasqualino's paradise had declined with the war and he had been forced to look for some kind of work that wasn't jeopardized by rationing. But no other job had ever succeeded in restoring that happiness he had known and was now reliving by recalling his life behind the counter of the butcher shop, high above the heads of others as on a throne.

"There was a colonel's maid who used to invent excuses to come in the shop several times a day; whenever she came in, the boss's wife would look at me from the cash register, wink with both eyes, and say, 'Go ahead, Pasqualino, go ahead and wait on the young lady!' And she'd come over and couldn't tear herself away; she kept looking at me and looking at me, and if she opened her mouth it was to tell me about her mistress—she always talked about her and not about herself. She told me how beautiful and elegant she was, that she had lots of admirers, that she had told her all about me, and that one day she herself would come to buy the meat. And in fact one day she did come; the boss's wife came out from behind the cash register and said to her,

her eyes popping out of her head, 'Good morning, signora, how come you're doing the shopping today?' 'I'm here to see this famous Pasqualino,' said the lady straight out. The boss's wife didn't know what to say and I kept looking in the other direction, but she came up to the counter, looked right at me, and laughed. She was a good-looking woman and the whole shop was already full of her perfume. 'I know you're an expert, Pasqualino. Why don't you cut me a nice roast, and I'll take it home myself?' Of course she knew that at that hour I'd have to go to the back of the shop to cut a roast. She followed right along, and while I was cutting the meat from the carcass, she said in a loud voice, 'You're so good at it, you know just where to cut.' Meanwhile she kept coming closer to me; she gave me a kiss at the corner of my mouth and laughed so much she couldn't stop. When she'd gone, the boss's wife called me over and said in a very serious way, 'Pasqualino, wipe the lipstick off your mouth and pay attention. It doesn't seem right to me, and besides her husband is a colonel.' 'What doesn't seem right?' I answered, but there really wasn't much I could say. The next day she called, she had me come to the phone, and asked me to bring another roast right away to her house. When I got there I found the maid, who was laughing and told me to go on in, the lady would pay me for the meat. But I got out of there as fast as I could, and as I went down the stairs, I said she could pay at her convenience."

"What a dope," Carlo said at this point.

"Dope or not, I blushed all over, and that's a fact!" Pasqualino replied in conclusion; then he started telling about the time when he'd worked as a cook. For the others, those were the happiest hours, but they filled me with a deep bitterness and made me sad.

Then someone at last would notice my silence. "Hey, you never talk about anything!"

"I have nothing to talk about," I replied, humiliated, and it was true.

Meanwhile, after the first days, I had learned many things: that you had to get up and stand at attention the minute you heard anyone approaching the door; if you weren't quick enough you were in trouble, for whether it was an ordinary guard or an officer who entered, if you weren't standing perfectly at attention, or if, even inadvertently, the sleeve of your jacket brushed against the wall, you got slapped hard and almost always kicked or hit with a stick besides.

Often, however, when the officers came to pay a visit, or a certain warrant officer who entered the cells with his pistol holster open as though he had to defend himself against some sort of attack, the blows were delivered for no particular reason—especially in cell 30, where there were two Italian generals and a colonel, of whom I'd once had a glimpse through a chink in the door, ragged, old, and on their last legs. Whenever the warrant officer entered cell 30, one always heard a loud sound of slapping, repeated more wildly and viciously if anyone protested. When calm returned and the guards had left, the question was heard from one of the other cells: "Who got it this time?"

"The general," was almost always the answer. Then someone would try to make a joke, and we would even laugh softly, without malice, only because it was all so sad and produced a pang in one's heart that could only be averted by a faint, good-natured smile.

On one of these days we had an important visit. Since morning the soldiers had come time and time again to the cells, along with the interpreter, a sixteen-year-old boy, to see that everything was in order, and to show us how we were to present ourselves, lined up by order of height, when the moment arrived.

"It's a very important high-ranking officer," the boy told us with his nasty smile. "You'd better be clean, orderly, and standing at attention. Don't speak unless spoken to: he's a high-ranking officer," and in saying "high-ranking officer," his moist, feminine lips curled in a contemptuous smile, which convinced me that what the others had told me was true: this kid was as cruel as they come.

We heard the high-ranking officer arrive, heard him proceeding from one cell to another, and at every stop there were savage outbursts, the sound of blows and riding crops, particularly accentuated at number 30. We heard all this just as we were getting ready to line up, and Carlo said, "It's the general again." We smiled, but it pained us.

At last the lock turned, and in came the high-ranking officer. He looked about twenty-five, short and slight, with a lieutenant's stripes, red hair, and bloodshot eyes; he wore a uniform blazing with the uniquely mechanical elegance of the Prussian soldier. He paused in the doorway, raised himself twice on tiptoe looking at us one by one, grimly, with his thin lips wrinkled and his eyes sharp under his red eyebrows. He came up to me, grabbed the collar of my shirt, thereby ripping off the button, and turned it back: it was dirty, for two weeks now I'd been unable to change my clothes, and already I'd been dragged through three filthy prisons.

"*Porco!*" he yelled in Italian. "Pig!" Then he started screaming like a madman in German; he stared in my eyes, started to go on to Piero who was standing beside me, turned back, put a hand on my shoulder, and flung me against the wall. Then he turned away, wiping his hand as though he had touched something foul. The others were cleaner than I since they'd been able to have their families send them some fresh clothes. After looking us all over one by one without sparing anyone an insult, he stooped to examine our things, namely a comb, a toothbrush, and a piece of soap for each; I still had nothing, except for a comb I had found there, and which I think had belonged to Giorgio Labò, who had preceded me in cell 31. With his fingertips he picked up this comb, saw it was dirty, and threw it out in the hallway, still yelling as though he would have liked to smash everything.

As the days went by in silence and darkness, we spent much of the time in a vague sadness, which was in direct proportion to the physical languor that increasingly took possession of us. But when the day was hectic, filled with insults or beatings, or even more the mournful groans of those coming back from the interrogations and often leaving a trail of blood in the corridor, our minds became glum, our faces hardened, and the silence seemed to petrify the air, defying any attempt to break it by those who tried not to feel overwhelmed. They were the worst moments, which only the solid and easygoing constitution of Carlo succeeded in overcoming: "Hey, guys, what'll we do? Want to go to the movies tonight?"

Someone answered decisively, "No, tonight we'll all stay home, we don't feel like going out."

"So okay, as you like." Then he would embark on his magical subject, his hobbyhorse. His hobbyhorse was Capri. He stood up, he was the oldest but the most stable of us all. He stood up, walked back and forth and began talking about his life on Capri, his youth as a seducer of blond Swedish or American girls who came there thinking they could paint. As for myself, I lingered more willingly in Pasqualino's butcher shop, but the others instead rolled their eyes and came to life; they went traveling with Carlo, with neither passport nor ticket, as he had done to New York, to the America of gangsters.

I preferred Pasqualino's butcher shop, or Piero's electrician's store, or else Luciano's stories, who when he spoke of his sweetheart or his mother would say every so often, as a refrain, while his almost angelic voice grew faint: "I'm still a kid, I'm younger than the rest of you." And as he said this he would gaze at me in dismay with his clear eyes, which by now almost took up his whole face, consumed by sixty days of hunger and darkness.

"All the grass under the sun is good," Luciano said one day while telling us about a walk on the outskirts of the city with his sweetheart. He wanted to explain to us how all of nature is good, to give us an idea of his naive faith in God, and it was painful for him to speak, while more than any of the rest of us he was diverted from the nightmare of the darkness by which we were enveloped.

I don't know why, but when Luciano spoke I was reminded of the nest of blackbirds that could be seen outside the window whenever one went to the bathroom. I had noticed it from the first moment I entered Via Tasso. At the top of a fir tree whose point came less than a meter from the bars on the window was this blackbirds' nest, and while the others brushed their teeth or did their business behind my back, I paused with my hands on the bars to look at the two little fledglings with their beaks open. Then the days went by and I saw them fly away at last over the roofs, toward the sky, followed by my facile sentimentality worthy

The World Is a Prison

of an old elementary-school primer. And yet, when I was able to linger to watch these free and lively creatures, before the German guard's *"Schnell! Schnell!"* forced us to run to avoid a beating, I returned to the darkness with a sense of relief; I felt I had breathed something that brought me a little light inside.

Threats Are Good for You

Every morning around eight the phones on the various floors started ringing, and each ring was a summons for an interrogation. When you went downstairs to be interrogated, you never knew in what state you'd come back—sometimes not on your own legs, but dragged by the head and feet by two soldiers and flung inside the cell like a sack, perhaps followed by a pail of ice-cold water if your wounds were such as to mess the floor with blood.

We each awaited our turn, but it generally came when you didn't expect it. That was how it happened to me. I was called while I was getting ready to go to the toilet: I was bare-chested, and just had time to put on my jacket with no shirt and go down the stairs under the watchful eyes of the sentries on the landings, who often gave you a violent shove to make you hurry.

For three days I was interrogated almost without interruption, except for the meal hour—three exhausting days that oddly enough gave me a kind of strength I seemed to have lost completely inside the cell. I felt wide awake, with a calm I was unable to account for, and even ready to react in a veiled and coolly polite fashion, whereby I noted, not without satisfaction, a certain disorientation on the part of my inquisitors. They grilled me unmercifully and tried all their tricks. Now they were courteous, even affable; now they called in a maniac whose chest was covered with medals and crosses; they put me face down on a desk and flogged me, laughing as though it were a game.

The one asking me questions wanted to be called Lieutenant Fritz. He was an elegant youth, perhaps an Italian, and translated everything I said for the German officer, who hour after hour never stopped staring at me, as though he might read something in my eyes.

From the first moment I began to realize that they meant to treat me in a special fashion, between cool and some-times strangely deferential politeness, and the anger and death threats that exploded furiously when I least expected it. If I had had to go through it earlier, I wouldn't have known what to think, I would have been unable to foresee my attitude; but I soon realized that the calmer I felt, the more terrible and peremptory the threats became. The more they threatened me with death, and especially when they brandished the bullwhip in my face, the more sure I came to feel that under no circumstances would I betray the friends whose names they wanted.

As soon as I entered the room, they sat me down in a corner next to a table on which five or six rawhide whips were lined up, some with wooden handles, others with ele-gant chrome-plated and engraved handles. As I sat down, the German officer did not look at me, but kept his eyes on these devices with the obvious intention of making me look at them too, and indeed I did turn and pretend to take an interest in them, while feeling at the same time, instinc-tively more than by any clear wish, that I was making an effort to assume a candid, serene, almost smiling expres-sion. I who in the simplest situations of life am often timid, and very often clumsy, felt strangely secure and self-pos-sessed. Except, deep within me, I had the terrible sensation that seems to become more acute in such circumstances than when one is alone in the darkness of the prison; I felt a sense of infinite solitude, the impression that the whole world had forgotten me, something that even today it occurs to me must be similar to what a shipwrecked person feels when alone and lost in the middle of the ocean. But this feeling was submerged, it lay hidden at the bottom of the soul; on the level of my nerves, never had I felt so alive and secure in an unwavering mood, whatever might happen.

I won't bother to recount the three days of interrogation, which anyway would resemble many that have been described by others. Compared with some I've heard of, I can today consider them three bland days, despite the alternating courtesies and beatings. Now it was a few lashes with the whip given like a ritual in the middle of the room, while I was held face down on a desk; now it was a cigarette, then even a coffee, and on the last day, before the final lashes on the soles of the feet, a cup of wine offered with the most pleasant of smiles.

The last time, after the courteous cup of wine, the German officer told them to inform me that in a few days I might be shot. I had been told this perhaps a hundred times, but this time, spoken with a courteous voice and in a tone of farewell, after I had signed my deposition, it made me think that it could really turn out that way. Today perhaps it astonishes me, but at that moment, and in all the days that followed, I entertained the idea with an indifference that caused me to analyze myself many times in the course of the day, trying to understand why it didn't make me suffer.

I was never able, however, to explain it, but I smiled to myself and concluded: "Good for you, Billy boy, I'm proud of you."

The World Is a Prison

Face to the Wall

"Now that you've signed the statement, all you can do is wait like we do, and God help us." This was what Piero said to me when I came back upstairs on the third day. But it didn't turn out that way; the next day I was called again, and as on the previous day, a noncommissioned officer in the SS came to get me at the door of the cell. This was something unheard-of in Via Tasso, it had never happened before, and the German guards looked at me in astonishment. I myself couldn't imagine to what to attribute this special treatment, but I think it had to do with the fact that I was an "intellectual," and as I'd been able to notice in my contacts with these people, they held those who in their opinion belonged to the so-called intellectual world in a kind of awe. So once again I was taken downstairs by my unusual escort, who with a bored smile let me go first through every door. They sat me down in an armchair in the same room, to one side instead of in the usual chair, offered me a cigarette, and there I waited for half an hour without knowing what I was supposed to do. Then they brought in a boy of twenty, one of the many very young prisoners, his eyes enhanced on his face by the long weeks in darkness; a stylish woman dressed in black immediately came in, followed by a man who must have been her husband. The minute they arrived, they threw their arms around the boy, and so for twenty minutes I witnessed a sad scene, the uninterrupted sobbing of a mother reunited with her trembling and exhausted son. He too wept; in his parents' presence he once more became a little boy letting himself be petted, and all of a sudden burst out in wails he was unable to contain. A sad scene, in short, which I witnessed from the side in silence, glad when the woman turned her tear-streaked face to me, stared me in the eyes, almost caressing me with her gaze, and it was as though she were my own mother looking at me. Then the three of them were rather rudely dismissed and the boy was sent back to his cell. I remained sitting for a while in the armchair with no one paying any attention to me; finally an officer came over, once again offered me a cigarette, and said, "You see, we can also be kind, we're human and try to understand other people's sufferings."

He gave me a light and I didn't answer. He stared at me for a moment, said something in German to the others, then motioned me to follow the usual noncommissioned officer, who took me back to my cell.

When he had left, the door was all of a sudden opened again, and the guard on our floor came in. He called me over to the doorway and asked haltingly, "How come you rate a special escort?"

"I don't know," I replied.

"You must be dangerous, you must have weapons." And with that he hit me so hard on the shoulder that it knocked me down. We all started laughing. Then those in the neighboring cells wanted to know what had happened and we had to tell them about it.

That evening, while we were sitting around silently, as was always the case toward evening, at a certain point we all found ourselves listening intently, holding our breath.

Something could be heard far away; we kept listening. It was the roar of big guns. For a long time we listened without saying a word; then Luciano tried to jump up and fell back, being especially unsteady on his feet. All the same he cried out: "They've come alive at Anzio. That's cannon fire!"

It was indeed the roar of a distant artillery barrage, powerful, monotonous, and similar to the thunder of distant storms. The faces of my four cellmates were radiant, they listened wide-eyed, and if someone started to say something, he was hushed by the others.

"Shut up! Otherwise we can't hear anything."

These were the first shellings on the Anzio front. I would never have thought, especially since after almost a year we had become accustomed to gunfire and explosions of every kind, that this distant roar would resound like a friendly appeal in the hearts of all those buried alive on Via Tasso. In the cells around us as well, we heard the inmates stirring, that hidden sort of rustle known to us by imperceptible noises, unusual movements, interrupted words. As they listened, all these prisoners, who a moment before had believed in nothing but the firing squad, now felt as though they were already free; some even dared to raise their voices from time to time: "They're coming! Airplanes have even flown over!"

But around ten o'clock, the usual dull sound of singing rose up from below, penetrating all the way to our cells. It was our jailers, who, as on almost every evening after dinner, were singing gloomy dirges. We all fell silent.

"They're still singing!"

"They won't sing for long."

"Don't fool yourselves," said a voice from a nearby cell.

"Maybe the Americans are really getting close," said someone else. "Don't forget, these people are even capable of killing us all before they leave. We'll have to find a way to defend ourselves!" These words were spoken in an emphatic tone.

"Who said that?" I asked Luciano, who knew all the voices.

"The general," he replied.

In the next days, toward evening, we often heard the shelling, and the same voices of hope were always raised here and there. But later came the mournful singing of the jailers.

During the days silence was our familiar enemy.

One evening they all ganged up on me because I never had any stories to tell. They grouped themselves around me, smiling and threatening: "You'd better tell us about something or we'll fix your wagon."

I really didn't know what to tell them, my past life seemed like such a vacuum. Then I remembered that before being arrested I had finished translating Alfred de Vigny's *Servitude et grandeur militaires,* and I thought of reciting the first of its three episodes. They gathered around and I started talking. By perhaps two or three in the morning I was still talking, often pausing to explain the meaning of some element in the story. They listened in silence; in the darkness I divined the wide-open eyes of my four friends and could feel them following me with rapt attention.

Always literature, I thought to myself—I'm nothing but a literary type. And this thought, which today is the only one able to sustain me, struck me as sad and empty.

That night we went to sleep later than usual; my story

had kept my audience extremely tense, though in the end they felt let down.

"That's not a happy ending," they told me.

I slept poorly, though we never slept very well anyway, because being locked up and inactive all day in the dark left us in a permanent state of somnolence while allowing us only brief intervals of real sleep. In the morning, as we were getting ready to go to the toilet, the same warrant officer came to summon me, indicating that I should take all my stuff with me. I collected my things without being able to glance at my companions; it was forbidden to say good-bye, or even to exchange words, and I left them standing there at attention and watching me in dismay.

I went downstairs accompanied by five other prisoners. No one knew where we were going: anything was possible. This exit could mean freedom (though there was little hope of that) or a firing squad, or being sent to dig trenches at Anzio, or merely a transfer to another prison.

They lined us all up and gave us back the objects that had been taken from us at the time we were jailed. An old man close by me, with stooping shoulders and extremely dirty, was crying like a baby and murmuring: "They're sending us home, they're sending us home . . ."

I looked at him, shaking my head. Tears ran down into his long, tangled Jewish beard, and fell on the lapel of his jacket and on the floor.

"They're sending us home," said others as well, but I had my doubts. They took us out to the street, and instead of letting us go made us get into a truck, guarded by four soldiers with submachine guns. We were driven across the city, and for a while I was distracted by again seeing people circulating freely in the streets. I was overcome by an incredible sadness, the like of which I had never felt so acutely during the twenty days of darkness, threats, and beatings. I was astonished to discover that I felt nostalgic for Via Tasso; I truly experienced, with deep and sincere simplicity, a great regret at leaving my four friends and emerging from that kind of void and moral silence in which I'd been sealed in cell 31. I disliked the idea of having to begin a new cycle all over again. I felt no curiosity for new things. The open air did not make me happy, and I thought: how can I be so weary of life?

We had arrived at the entrance to Regina Cœli, and I was only aware of it when the driver slammed on the brakes, jolting and toppling us one against another.

It must have been noon when, after having been marched through a series of gates, halting first in a court-yard, then in the rotunda from which the various wings branched out, I was taken to the Third Wing, the forbidden sector of Regina Cœli, where no Italian had ever been admitted unless he was a prisoner, and left standing with my face to the wall. For a short while, next to me and in the same position, they also left the old Jew, who went on weeping, looking upward in a strange invocation to his God; then he was taken away and I was alone. I was tired, my legs hardly held up, and I began to feel how much I had been affected by the hunger, darkness, and lassitude of Via Tasso. I had already been perhaps an hour in this position when I decided to turn around and at least get some idea of where I was. Not far above my head was the first tier of the wing's three levels with its row of innumerable cell doors; they all had their grilles open and behind them one could see women's faces. No sooner had I turned around than they all began making desperate signs to me; at first I didn't understand, then I realized they were imploring me to turn back to the wall. "Don't turn around!" the woman closest to me hissed. "Do you hear me? Don't turn around or they'll beat you up." Thus I realized that the same laws applied in the Third Wing as in Via Tasso, and again turned my face to the dirty wall, listening to the comings and goings behind my back.

And hours went by without anyone paying any attention to me. Every so often I flexed my legs and with an effort resumed my position, always tempted to let myself fall to the floor. But I knew very well it would do no good, and that the only result would be kicks and blows from the jailers who were going back and forth armed with whips, riding crops, and truncheons.

With my eyes turned to the wall and the growing sensation of navigating in space, increasingly oppressed by a nightmare full of the classic sounds of prison, I spent the last hours dazed and sluggish, assailed from time to time by thoughts and memories hitherto remote. All of a sudden I realized that for the first time I was thinking of my mother; it seemed to me that so far an instinctive mental impulse had kept dismissing memories, the memory of people dear to me. It occurred to me that from the first moments I had spent in a cell—and by now it was almost a month—I had been making an effort, partly instinctive and partly deliberate, to detach myself from whatever might be a sentimental tie with "life outside," the life I had to consider lost, and God only knew if I would ever regain it. I thought of my mother, and amid the greasy spots on the wall that for hours on end were before my eyes I distinctly saw the cherished haunts of my native city, and actually felt I recognized the signs of a few smiles that until now I had so shrewdly banished from my mind. The narrow, twisting streets of my city appeared submerged in a luminous night and shifted slowly as on a screen, one after another, along with a swarm of thoughts and worries that frightened me. So far I hadn't thought of my parents, who perhaps knew where I was, and suddenly I realized that for many years I had ceased thinking about such ties; I had no longer felt them as part of myself nor felt they were necessary. What had my life been until now? Why at this point did I find myself here? Was it by a quirk or for some eccentric act that I had ended up in the hands of such unspeakably horrible human creatures?

And my thoughts ran dizzily on, as though all of a sudden, having with difficulty left my past far behind without ever looking back, I was now churning around inside it, sliding in no time into the saddest and fondest moments of my existence. Suddenly a woman's voice behind me carried me back to a certain street that I hadn't seen and hadn't remembered since I was a child; I had a clear vision of certain rainy days I had spent on that street as a boy, under an arcade on which the windows of my house opened—those long days spent looking at the gutter, where the water from outside ran in the middle of the pavement under the arch and was swallowed up by the sewer. It was in those moments that the boy I was had already begun listening to himself, and discovering the strange and contradictory depths of his nature. It was in those moments that I realized that a kind of strength and imaginative fervor arose within me amid the idleness of boring days, filled with rain and silence; it was in those times and those places that I realized how it pained me to understand, how I felt I understood too much, and how in that pain I felt a nagging rebellion, which kept growing within me, the only riches granted me by a life of poverty and solitude.

Why was I here? Why did I need to ask? And it was then that I seemed to discern in myself a conflict that, having simmered in my heart since my early youth, had found its natural resolution in the events in which I had participated along with all those I had chosen, in the course of my life, as friends and working companions. There it was: my life, which I had always thought a revolt against only myself, imagining its inner and solitary development in almost every one of its acts, had a meaning that linked it to the lives of others. My private and particular rebellion was a protest always repulsed by a hostile world, but it had found a way, when common sufferings and moral disasters had emerged from our individual hearts, to identify itself with many others. Had the war therefore been necessary?

Regina Cœli

Finally they came to search me, once again taking away everything I had. For the last time I saw my wallet containing all my assets, my necktie, my leather belt, my rock-crystal eyeglasses, the mechanical pencil my girlfriend had given me, my pen, and I don't know how many other things to which I'd become inordinately attached, as often happens to me with small objects.

I was then taken to cell 333, on the third floor. Before admitting me, the German posted a card with my name under two others and asked me, "Are you married?"

"No." He shook his head and shoved me inside.

I stayed near the door, which creaked shut behind me, looking at the two young men who were standing in the middle of the room. My temples were pounding, and I was seeing people and objects as in a mist; in the end, overcome by fatigue, I threw myself supine on a straw pallet. The two of them had remained silent, looking at each other with oddly frightened faces.

When, after resting a bit, I tried to look around, it seemed to me I was in a delightful place: at the rear was a big window from which one could see a good stretch of sky; on the floor were three filthy pallets, but still it wasn't the bare floor; against the walls were shelves, which gave me a comfortable feeling, and scattered here and there were wooden spoons, tin cans, a few books, some sheets of paper and a pencil, some tobacco, and a pack of cards.

"But this is the lap of luxury," I said.

"Where the devil did you drop from?" my two new companions seemed to be saying as, still silent, they scrutinized me. One of them was a pallid boy with a little gold chain around his neck, a fresh, clean silk shirt, a pair of elegant and pressed trousers, and slender hands; the other one was also quite young, exceedingly blond, with clear and candid eyes, wearing only a torn shirt and a pair of dirty pants. The first turned out to be the only son of a noble Roman family, he was here almost en passant; the other was a Pole from Warsaw who had been digging trenches for two or three years on all the fronts in Europe.

That day I ate meat and sweets, drank coffee, and became so cheerful that I felt obliged to tell the other two how I had been living for the past weeks, since otherwise they would have been unable to account for my mood. The Pole did not speak Italian, so while I talked, the other translated my words into German. All these God-given delicacies came from the house of the young Roman, for among other things, in Regina Cœli, one was allowed to receive a food package from one's family twice a week.

Toward evening I had my first unpleasant sensation on noticing the legion of bedbugs that slowly and inexorably came crawling down the wall in the direction of the pallets on which we would have to spend the night; for a moment I was afraid I would throw up. But we started a three-handed card game and I forgot about it until the time came to go to sleep. The boy with the gold chain was sent home, and he was replaced by a character who, despite all my goodwill, I found so disgusting for the whole time he was with us that I forgot the bedbugs, which every morning left our cheeks and our whole bodies bloody since we crushed them by the hundreds by moving in our sleep. This was a huge and very old man, with wrinkled skin that looked like terra-cotta; in every wrinkle he had a black furrow of dirt and his hands were literally encrusted with who knows how many decades of filth. Shortly after his arrival, the cell was invaded by flies, which alighted by the dozen on his drooping shoulders to attack his neck, face, and arms. He sat there all day, groaning about the flies that didn't let him sleep and slapping his arms, face, and neck to squash them on his skin. For me every time he swatted himself was like a punch in my stomach, and I always felt I was about to vomit. In vain did I protest inwardly against this truly misplaced sensitivity—it was stronger than I. I felt I was living with a big ape, and turned as much as possible to the Pole, who talked constantly, without my understanding a word. He spent half the day stark naked, perhaps aware of his perfect body, perhaps conscious that his beauty was a source of benevolence on the part of our jailers.

Then the old man was also taken away, and for a couple of days I was left alone with the Pole.

The first two days I was in cell 333 I took pains to fulfill a wish that had come to me on seeing the pencil. I wanted to write notes about my experiences, but I had to get hold of some paper. So I began collecting all the pieces of wrapping paper I could get my hands on; they were yellow, blue, white, any color at all, but by folding and carefully tearing them, I produced some little slips all more or less the same size on which I could write. On the morning of 24 May I already had about twenty of them and was ready to begin a sort of diary.

But I was surprised to find how the wish vanished as soon as I was in a position to carry it out. Thus once again I realized that in prison one creates wishes that do not correspond to necessity but serve only as distraction, especially when it takes long and patient effort to fulfill them.

I had the paper, I had the pencil, but I had no idea what to write. Still, I managed to jot down a few lines every day, and on rereading them today, I have the feeling that they convey sufficiently the atmosphere of the Third Wing, though for some reason or other any mention of actual events would seem to have been expressly avoided, in order to dwell only on certain states of mind and certain less noteworthy details.

By transcribing these slips of paper here, and adding what I remember of those thirteen more days, I can fill out this book, at least until the day when the Allied armies entered Rome. The first of them, dated 24 May, reads as follows:

> 5 persons left this morning, as always at the same hour, and everyone expects it to be himself.

In fact, since the first morning I had learned that almost at dawn every morning the SS arrived with lists, made the rounds of the designated cells, and took away a number of unfortunates who shortly thereafter, as we knew, ended up before a firing squad at Forte Boccea. At that hour, everyone was nervous, very few felt secure until these devils had gone past their cell, and when once in a while they paused uncertainly at yours to read the occupants' names posted on the door, you saw faces go pale, while all around there was silence. In accordance with my usual levity, I managed not to get scared, and said to myself every morning, without any particular emphasis, that if they were to call me I'd actually feel nothing extraordinary—actually nothing, I repeated in my heart, to convince myself it was true. Every time the scene was enacted, I went to the grille in the cell door to see the faces of those who had been called, and among the things I find it hard to forget is the image of those I saw leaving. They were all smiling as they came out of their cells; it was a smile not easily forgotten, a sad smile, but a smile nonetheless.

My notes for that day continue:

> Found a bedbug on my shirt, am beginning to get used to them, since it didn't have much effect on me, while two days ago just seeing them on the wall made me feel sick to my stomach.

> The guard grabbed me by the chest and knocked me against the wall because I hadn't started cleaning up.

Cleaning up meant sweeping the floor and emptying the pot in which we relieved ourselves during the night—our W.C., so to speak—into a garbage can that the janitors hauled from door to door. The next note reads:

> Here I'm better off, and my appetite has come back, and yet for some reason or other there are times when I still miss the hell of Via Tasso, maybe because of the friends with whom I got along so well, maybe because there were no bedbugs there, despite having to sleep on the floor.

> Here the blankets disgust me and for the moment I can't overcome it.

> The Pole talks and talks, he bores me, and I don't understand a word he says.

The next day, while waiting for the first package of victuals that some kind soul never let me go without all the time I was in Regina Cœli, I wrote on my slips of paper:

> I can't explain how it is that I feel so calm and never think of freedom; there are times when the hours here even seem pleasant to me.

Every so often, with a few gestures, I communicate to the Pole my anger at being locked up; but I'm not sincere, my real feeling is of waiting without worrying about it. My mind wanders all day long, I feel I wouldn't be able to write a line.

One of my most important wishes, ever since I've been in prison, is to look at myself in the mirror. I'm afraid I must be very run down, and am curious to see myself with a long beard.

Here I've found some books I would never have dreamed of reading and instead I read an average of three every two days. These books depress me, but since reading makes the time go by without one realizing it, I read them.

Here are some titles: *Il triangolo d'oro* by Countess . . . ; *The Four Just Men* by Edgar Wallace; *L'anima si spegne* by Zihaly; *A tu per tu con l'amore* by Luigi Nanni Pieri; *La seconda notte* by Adriano Baracco.

In the next cell I had glimpsed the cover of a volume in the "Medusa" series and couldn't wait to get my hands on it. Finally I succeeded. It was Alain-Fournier's *Le Grand Meaulnes,* which was passed along to me with *Per un bacio* by Flavia Steno.

In my career as a reader it was Alain-Fournier who was to move me the most. And it is from the feelings produced by reading that book that I'm able to deduce my true state of mind, since in what I was able to think I found nothing in myself but indifference toward everything that might happen to me—toward the prison, toward that shadow of death that, along with the heavy tread of two or three SS guards, every morning grazed the hundreds of prisoners in the Third Wing. It means I have all the apprehensions and anxieties that would be natural, but they're hidden even from myself and look for other ways, I thought, when in reading that fine book in a bad Italian translation I was seized by an inner agitation I had never felt before.

On the slip for 26 May I wrote something about it:

> I recall the moment when I saw the first bedbug on the wall of this cell the morning of the 21st. How disgusted I felt! And now after an interval of five days I don't pay much attention, not even when I find them in my clothes or on the bread. Too bad that one gets used to everything, but in a way we're lucky.

Now comes an interruption: I had started reading.

> I've had to stop at the chapter about the death of Yvonne de Galais. I've never been so moved by a book. I got all choked up and the book produced an immense emotion in my heart, which seemed as though it would suffocate since I found no room for it in the cell. I'll recover in a while and start reading again.

Two days after the departure of the man being devoured by flies, the Pole and I had a new cellmate in Bellarmino, a plumber; he too had come from Via Tasso. Threatened more than once with death, he was always on his guard, more anxious than frightened, and during this time I observed a sensibility in him that I had either lost or was unable to find in myself. Unwittingly he kept an ear cocked at every moment, and at every unusual noise his little restless eyes were fixed on the door. He was a good cardplayer, spoke little, and recalled dead Germans and Fascists with an indifferent simplicity that I found daunting.

The evening when, at a quite unusual hour, I heard my name at the door, I saw Bellarmino jump up from his pallet and turn pale; his hands were trembling. Outside the door they kept muttering and saying my name, and it really was something out of the ordinary. I reacted with apathy, and didn't bother to look up from reading *Il colpevole perde la partita* by Edmondo Fink. Actually, they were looking for me in order to bring me a food package, delivering it at a strange hour without the usual procedure, and I've never understood why. Nor did I ever learn who sent it to me, but it had to be someone who didn't know me at all, since I ended up giving the entire contents to my two cellmates.

"When I heard them call your name I went weak in the knees," Bellarmino said on this occasion, smiling with his row of little close-set teeth.

He's still alive, I thought.

On 27 May I was finally able to look at myself in the mirror. It may not seem like much, but when at the barber's I saw for a moment, only a moment, my face with several centimeters of beard, I felt the joy of someone realizing a wish that had been thwarted for years. I paused to consider my new appearance and even found it flattering; then the barber flayed me alive, hacking away at me without mercy.

By 29 May everyone in the Third Wing was restless. First there seemed to be a kind of uneasiness in the air, then in moments when the guards weren't watching there was more and more talk from one cell to another through the grilles. "They're just a few kilometers from Rome. They've got beyond Anzio!" Everyone said the same thing, and from time to time it was confirmed by increasingly heavy and closer shelling. Nervousness mounted, and while in Via Tasso hearts had opened at the sounds of battle, here they induced worry on all faces and anxiety in all voices. Perhaps it was because the closer the roar of artillery came, the more one noticed a certain agitation among the German police who garrisoned the prison and formed the guard in our wing. Insults and beatings diminished in frequency during these days, and some Germans who always made the rounds with sticks in their hands were seen going back and forth along the galleries without their weapons. But the greatest anxiety came from the fact that some were convinced that we in the Third Wing would shortly be collected en masse and transported outside Rome. This prospect, certainly not unfounded and ever more certain the closer the fall of Rome seemed, caused great anxiety in everyone. Some prisoners paced up and down in their cells, or let out intermittent cries, and in the silence that almost always descended on us toward evening, we sometimes heard a shout: "*Viva l'Italia!*"

This shout sounded strange in the prison, in the increasing silence that enveloped the vast vault of the Third Wing, under which several hundred men and women, and even a few children, electrified the air with their mood, as much by their silence as by their unusual agitation. In me, as always, the general atmosphere produced the opposite reaction; the more I felt anxiety and agitation around me, the calmer I became, not to say indifferent. On a slip of paper for that day I wrote in the first lines:

> All day today we've heard shelling that never let up; all the prisoners are nervous and, now when it looks like we're at the end, afraid of being taken away; actually I'm afraid of it myself; my mood, however, is excellent and I'm satisfied with my nature.

The next sentence in this note is likewise owing to my ever reactive mood. Seeing how everyone at this time was thinking only of his own situation and of what might shortly happen, as if nothing mattered but what happened in those days—though basically it was very natural to think so—caused me to add:

I'm also satisfied because, despite my personal situation, I think of Rome as an episode in the war; were I to think only of my own convenience I'd be guilty of unjustifiable selfishness in view of everything I've gone through so far.

In the following days the general agitation increased. All those who had been in prison, often for many months, without ever having been interrogated were called during the night until four or five in the morning, while the shelling came closer and became heavier and more persistent. At intervals it seemed to stop and one saw a nervousness—which was actually raw torment in the more excitable—in everyone's eyes; but then the shelling resumed and a sudden silence fell: everyone was listening.

With the stepped-up pace of the interrogations, we heard of new death sentences.

On 1 June they came to take the Pole away, as they told him, to work with the Todt. Then in the evening came a moment when we opened all the cell doors and went out on the landings; the locks in the Third Wing were broken, and if we hadn't been afraid of a beating, we could have gone out anytime we liked. That evening we all stayed outside for an hour and no one came to threaten us or ran out to yell at us. Then a few men in German uniforms showed up; we already knew they weren't the same ones as before, and that all the guards had been replaced. These new ones approached and with the utmost courtesy asked us to go back into our cells: we could scarcely believe our eyes. In the end we learned that these were German soldiers from the Alto Adige and that almost all of them spoke Italian. Of course, this change meant something to us all; but the interrogations continued one after another, as though all of a sudden the Germans were in a hurry. That night I wasn't sleepy, and toward four o'clock was trying to get some air at the door, which for some reason had been left ajar; a guard went by and I started to draw back out of habit, instinctively expecting to see his stick appear between the bars. Instead the soldier looked in through the opening, smiled at me, and said in good Italian: "What a drag, eh? It's a lousy place."

I nodded and went back to my bug-infested pallet.

In the morning, a noncommissioned guard officer came to call me around seven o'clock, mangling my name in an incredible way; I wanted to have a look at his paper to make sure he meant me. Bellarmino stared at me with eyes that even seemed to grow large; he looked at me but lacked the courage to speak.

"I'm the one who has to go, you see?" I told him, and he nodded without saying a word. I knew what he was think-ing, and certainly the hour and the way I'd been called were not exactly reassuring. Nevertheless, I followed the German with a light-enough heart, though I was more con-vinced than ever that this might be my last day. As always happened, heads poked out of all the cells, at the little win-dows in the doors, to see who it was who was "leaving"; I saw hundreds of eyes watching me and read in all those faces a dismay that perhaps resembled my own when each morning, like them, I saw someone being taken away; the expression of those faces, cut in four by the two crossed bars in the grilles, seemed to dispel all my own dismay. I've succeeded in being like this to the end, I thought.

In the room where I was taken, soldiers and officers were seated or standing, while two other prisoners, rigid, with strained faces, stood at attention in the middle of the floor.

I was placed alongside them and ordered to stand at attention. The soldiers around us were talking mostly among themselves or tying their shoes; but a lieutenant and a non-commissioned officer started walking around us, brandishing thin leather riding crops in our faces and repeating with coarse laughter, while with their hands they went through the motions of firing a gun: "Bang-bang! Bang-bang!"

How many times by now I had seen this gesture made and heard this exclamation! Their behavior convinced me even more of our destiny, but still I felt sadly indifferent. In a moment of calm I asked the man next to me: "Where are we going? What did you do?"

"I've been sentenced to die. Where we're going I don't know," he replied in proper Italian but with a German accent. I wasn't able at the moment to ask him anything else, but now there seemed to be no need for further clarification.

Instead I was wrong, as I found out while they were taking us outside to board a truck with an abundant escort of submachine guns. Passing close to the interpreter, who knew me and perhaps had come near me on purpose, I was able to ask him, "Where are they taking me?"

Almost without moving his lips so as not to be seen talking to me, he whispered, "To the tribunal."

The day before, this man had succeeded in bringing me in the cell greetings from M., and to receive a greeting from "outside" after so many weeks, a simple greeting, had made me so happy that I now looked on him fondly, as though he had actually brought me freedom.

In the truck we were able to talk. The third one was a child, a kid who didn't look more than sixteen, tattered, dressed in the rags supplied by the prison to those who had nothing, rags so torn and filthy that his bones stuck out everywhere. He had very clean, slender hands, a simple and childish profile, his oval face barely covered by a light blond down. He spoke in a soft, deep voice, and told me in a few words that he was the son of the stationmaster of a village near Bari, that he had crossed the lines on an assignment he didn't specify to me, and that on his return he had been caught because a mine had exploded at his feet; saying this, he pointed to one of his legs, all swathed in bloody bandages, and explained that he still suffered a lot of pain, which he didn't have to say because you could see it from his face as he spoke.

The other, who had been sentenced to death, was a German deserter, but he spoke Italian perfectly; he couldn't understand why they were taking him back to the tribunal since that was where he had been sentenced a few days before.

The German military tribunal was in a sumptuous villa in a high-class neighborhood. We had to wait a few hours in the anteroom. First the deserter was called, and came back with his sentence commuted to hard labor; then it was the boy's turn. Limping and ragged, he went through the imposing glass door that led to the other rooms, smiling with the handsome face of an intelligent boy, with the slender and elegant carriage of a simple and civilized Italian, which even despite his rags could not be overwhelmed by the luxurious yet rather vulgar ostentation of the place. He came back smiling and I thought he was pleased. He sat down next to me, looking at me for a long time without speaking.

"Well?" I asked him.

"The firing squad," he replied, without lowering his

head. There was a tremor in his voice and his eyes clouded over, but he did not lower his gaze, and I was ashamed of myself for having feared he would waver; he was steady and endearing, under the weight of that sentence that seemed so inappropriate on his childish lips that kept trying not to tremble.

In a salon with large cut-glass windows and ten or twelve polished marble columns behind a huge portrait of Hitler draped with swastika banners, six German officers, flanking a general or something of the kind, were sitting around a horseshoe table covered with other swastika flags. On close examination, the solemn purpose of this display had the air of a village fair, and the stiff, impeccable characters, their legs tangled in the red flannel of the flags, looked like a parody of the old Prussian spirit. Stroheim couldn't have done better.

"Come forward," I was told. I took a few steps toward the table.

"One step back."

Then the man in the middle stood up and said a few words that made the others jump to their feet and stand at attention in the incredible German way. Next came several minutes of getting up and sitting down. Finally one told me I was in the presence of the judges of the German military tribunal and that I was allowed to reject one of them.

"Let them stay." They all smirked.

Then they debated among themselves for half an hour, but I understood nothing. I even think the last one who got up may have spoken in my defense. They carried on so seriously that I was flooded by a sense of the ridiculous, as when one is ashamed of the stupidity of others.

In the end I was told, in Italian, that I would have to

serve ten years of forced labor in some mine or other in Germany. I knew what that meant and continued to stand there, as though what was happening did not concern me. The truth is I had the feeling that all this was something that had nothing to do with me.

They went out, and I waited there for half an hour. Finally they came back and took their places, repeating the ritual of standing up and sitting down again; then they informed me that the ten years had been reduced to five.

Since I gave no sign of life, the officer sitting in the middle had them ask me, "Are you satisfied?"

"Of course I'm not satisfied," I replied candidly. Then he got up indignantly, yelling curses at me that echoed in the room, and extending his clenched hands toward my person as if to reach me and scratch me.

"Get out!" he said. And I was taken back to the others.

In the street the boy had little to say. I tried to speak to him but my words were trite; we heard, however, the sound of artillery quite close and I called his attention to it. He looked at me gratefully, it really cheered him up a little, then again he was lost in thought. As I watched him, it seemed to me that images were passing before his eyes, and I left him to contemplate his private world without knowing what to say to him. I saw him taken away, docile and silent, to a separate cell, and tried several times to say good-bye, but he didn't see me. He was such a little kid.

The next day, at a certain point, I wrote on one of my slips of paper:

> . . . a few minutes ago I reproached myself for not having thought much about the kid who is down there alone pondering his imminent death and suffering from his still-unhealed foot. I said to myself, "But what's the point of thinking about him?" Truly, my thinking about him doesn't

do him any good; I ended, however, by considering this argument somewhat less than honest and really thought about his sadness.

Anyway, though it doesn't do him any good, it's still important that I think about and mull over this matter instead of evading it: man enriches himself in the consideration of things, and the enrichment of a mind in sharing the sufferings of others, even minimally, is not an end in itself; so nothing is lost, we are instruments of a consciousness whose importance goes well beyond our individuality.

I spent the hours of that day lying on my pallet looking at the walls; there was an unusual confusion all around, the battle far away was unremitting and seemed to be coming rapidly closer; the shelling never let up.

There were numerous inscriptions, curious and obscene, on the walls of the cell, but over my head was written: "Here lies Aldo Piperno sentenced for being born. Born 26.10.1913 died . . ." That "sentenced for being born" made a certain impression on me. But over the pallet where I lay there was this, written with indelible pencil: "Alfredo Vacca, son of Gennaro and of Nunzia Maggio. Born 25.3.1926 in Naples. Arrested 17.4.1943 in Naples, accused of 5 burglaries in houses of bomb victims—committed during air raids—15 years of hard labor—Don't be afraid of hard labor, boys, they don't eat people."

After copying these inscriptions onto my slips of paper, I finally tried to account for the unusual excitement. I looked out the grille, which was now almost always open; the new guards didn't care, just as they didn't care about the loud conversations that went on from one cell to another. Someone had heard the news that the Americans were supposed to be close. "Let's hope they don't suddenly decide to take us away," everyone said at the end of any conversation.

The next day, however, they started evacuating the Third Wing. In a first roll call 150 prisoners were singled out and taken below to be sent north. This was bad news, and I received it by immediately starting to think of something else; I didn't do so deliberately, but by now I was quite conscious of the instinctive ways whereby I spared myself the slightest anxiety. But toward evening, almost all of them came back, to a raucous welcome from a hundred throats hidden behind the doors.

"How come you're back?" I asked one who was nearby.

"Because they don't have any transport vehicles. We've seen a lot of confusion." And so saying, the sprightly old man I had asked performed a leap and a pirouette that I could only envy.

"Something's going to happen tomorrow morning," everyone said. It was the third of June.

"333"

When I woke up on the morning of 4 June, I was struck by some amusing coincidences of my prison days. I waited for Bellarmino to turn his head toward me and told him, "Something's bound to happen today, maybe we'll really get out."

"Let's hope," he said, his dark, blinking eyes lighting up with hope and disbelief. "But why?" he added.

"Look," I explained, "I was arrested on May third, I'm in cell 333, I've been in prison for thirty-three days, I'm in the Third Wing, I'm thirty-three years old. I've been in three prisons, not counting the cell in the police station; the number of my cell in Via Tasso was thirty-something; the interrogations I went through lasted three days, and there may still be other threes that I can't think of. So today, rightly speaking, we should get out, so that the last whole day I spend in prison will be day three, which is yesterday's date." Bellarmino laughed.

When daylight came we realized that not one German could be seen or heard in the wing. An hour passed quietly, then one of the janitors started going from cell to cell, saying, "Get ready." Behind him rose cries, questions, murmurs that grew louder and almost threatening.

"Who told you we should get ready?" I asked the janitor.

"None of your business," he replied and went on. Actually, the confusion kept getting louder, and if it could arrive at this point, it meant there was really no longer any surveillance. Little by little we were all out on the landing. The air force captain in the cell almost opposite mine started giving orders, went below, and came back up, yelling, "Keep calm! Keep calm!" as though he were on the deck of a sinking ship. But now no one tried to keep calm. I went back in my cell and made up a bundle of my stuff, not forgetting the wooden spoon, which I'd decided to take with me.

When it looked as though we ought to start going down to the ground floor, we saw two German guards emerge from the stairs on the side. The mob of prisoners who by now had poured out on the landings wavered in fear, there was a moment of panic, but the two guards approached cautiously, even timidly, with conciliatory smiles. They begged us to go back in our cells: "Just for a little while, a little while," they said. But seeing how compliant they were, no one cared to obey, until that same air force captain came and, cursing, urged us to go back inside for a while. We all went back, but no one would close his door.

Bellarmino kept walking back and forth in the cell, clutching his bundle of rags.

"Let's have a game of cards," I said. But he looked at me as though he thought I'd gone crazy.

"Don't worry. Thirty-three, three hundred thirty-three, the numbers are infallible, we're getting out today." I was convinced of it. Bellarmino, however, was nervous.

Since there was nothing else to do, I started writing a new slip of paper:

10 A.M.: This morning they passed the word: get ready. Then great general commotion, then all the cells being opened and people saying it would be any moment now. Great commotion, but we don't understand a thing. It's ten o'clock and we're still here.

A few minutes ago someone ran by and said, "They're at Ciampino!"

In short, according to what we heard yesterday, they're waiting for action from outside. Will it fail? Will it be one more delusion? We keep waiting.

I had just written "We keep waiting" when I heard a great uproar: it was all the prisoners rushing out of the cells and stampeding down the stairs. Bellarmino was already out and I followed him. On the ground floor of the Third Wing an enormous crowd surged toward the gate of the central dome, which was still closed.

"You're killing yourselves!" someone shouted desperately, but now no warning was of any use. All I could see around me were flushed faces and, up ahead, a furious struggle to get out. Above, on the several balconies of the wings where the ordinary criminals were housed, there was another raging crowd: the atmosphere was like a pit in hell, and I thought how each of these men, so as to be the first to arrive at the narrow gates where no more than two or three could pass at a time, was ready to kill his neighbor if only to get out ten seconds earlier.

At last we were all in the rotunda under the dome, amid the howls of the regular prisoners trying to get out with us. At one point the commotion was convulsive, and a submachine gun was fired from somewhere, making holes in the wall a few meters above our heads. My first thought was that they were firing to calm things down, but the struggle grew hellish as the nonpolitical prisoners broke through and mingled with us. Standing on the sidelines, I could tell them apart just by looking at them; there was something in the faces of the "politicals" that unmistakably distinguished them from the others. But if it was theoretically easy for me to tell one from the other, it was no longer possible for the

Italian jailers, who were submerged and trampled by the infuriated crowd milling around the narrow exit gates and unable to make any progress.

Gunshots, curses, bruises, furious struggles were centered with increasing violence at the door, and I stood aside along with two or three others who were quietly waiting until we could leave without being crushed. An hour went by, and at a certain moment, almost without knowing how, I was among the first ones out, leaving behind me an atmosphere of tragedy. As I set out for the main entrance, I turned and saw the interpreter, his jacket ripped in two, vainly trying to separate the "politicals" from the others, while two guards from the municipal police force threatened to shoot into the melee if things didn't calm down.

Through the Streets, in a House

No sooner do you step outside a prison than you look up: you look at the sky.

I went out and passed into the midst of a shouting crowd, some of whom were clapping their hands. I walked quickly away and crossed the Ponte Mazzini. I don't know what I'd been expecting outside, but the sight of Germans still guarding the bridge disoriented me. What, we're out and there are Germans? I really couldn't figure it out.

But still farther along on the Tiber embankment, and walking under the plane trees, I was able to relax. I stopped and, leaning on the parapet, looked at the water in the river. Overhead the perfect sky of Rome curved above the Janiculum; there was so much space up there, so much greenery down here; the Red Circle trams were jammed one against another, unable to move.

At the Ponte Sisto I stopped again, in the grip of a boundless sadness. Life seemed to me miserable. So what is it I want? I wondered. I was free and it gave me no satisfaction: quite the contrary, and now I began to understand how I had been oppressed by endless regrets on setting foot outside the prison on Via Tasso, something that little by little I'd identified as a kind of nostalgia for days spent equally, slowly, full of boredom and somnolence in prison cells. I tried to understand why I should be suffering from such feelings, and it was as though a kind of void had opened in me on emerging from Regina Cœli.

Yes, indeed! I thought. I was better off inside those narrow walls and with no way out; there was something in me there that now has already vanished. Now I'm back among people! This last thought filled me with anxiety, as though being once more part of a free life were a greater burden than being inexorably cut off from it.

It was only when I was in the bathtub at a friend's house, feeling the physical delight of being immersed in warm water and the clean scent of soap, that all of a sudden I felt the bitterness that had filled me with anxiety being dispelled.

Toward evening, I watched from the window as the last German passed along the street close to the outskirts of the city. He came from the direction of the sea, covered with grime, his face streaked with it, stooping under the weight of several cartridge belts; he walked with slow and limping steps, at times seemingly overwhelmed by the utmost fatigue. He was the last man in a column of twenty others like himself; completely undone, they had a look of final, sad awareness. It was a sight that expressed only animal sadness, the sadness of oxen on their way to the slaughterhouse.

They hadn't yet arrived at the end of the avenue when from my balcony I saw the first American tanks emerge from behind the Pyramid of Cestius: the same tired, muddy faces, but these were smiling.

So what was I supposed to think? I don't think it's too much to say I didn't know. Who could have been more bewildered than many of us at that time? I know that a new life is now beginning, I thought. May my thirty-three years now bring me something I should have had since birth and instead have never had. But what it might be, I certainly didn't know. I felt that my experiences had not been enough for me even to take the first step toward what everyone was already calling freedom, to which, among other things, I was bringing a life that needed to be completely remade. I had nothing left but a few friends and the wooden spoon with which I had tried, unsuccessfully, to eat the soup of prisoners. Already at that moment I was feeling what in the months to come would seem to me the simplest truth: that the immense cycle of wars and social tragedies around us was not only around us but in the most secret part of our lives, amid our most private interests. Anyone who had a woman would not find her the same; anyone who had a house would find it different; anyone with a heart would approach it again like an unfamiliar guest, who would need to look carefully around him before knowing where he was and occupying the place himself.

In the streets, in the so-called salons, at meetings, in the midst of the crowd that "exulted" without knowing exactly about what, it was increasingly clear that there was no point seeking new support in one's surroundings, or new equilibrium for one's faltering steps. And yet almost all of us were searching outside ourselves, in the streets, in the words of others. But the first step toward life can only be taken by starting from the depths of one's soul, of one's culture, of the experience that represents in each of us the age-old feeling of tradition and our history, and only by discovering in ourselves the meaning of things born around us, of the feelings that emerge and evolve.

No, despite appearances, I felt I understood that nothing would be able to arise from outside, nothing could come from others, if each of us did not first have the courage to go and dig to the depths of our own souls, to the origins of our historical period. Only a moral solution could bring me and my friends, my contemporaries, my fellow Italians, onto a new path. And humans find a moral solution only by seeking, in their own feelings, in the sentiments buried in the depths of their hearts, the universal truths bearing the marks of the tragedies that surround them.

So the more I saw others looking anxiously here and there for something to do, the new house in which to live, the more I, no longer having anything, felt the need to look only into my heart, into my inner life (something incapable of giving me even a mouthful of bread) for a new equilibrium, a new justification for the need to live, and the will to join somehow in the sufferings and joys of others.

Postscript (1960)

At fifteen years' distance my children find it hard to understand: describing the events doesn't do much good, one has to communicate the feelings, and then a few results can be seen. One needs to transmit the ideas. These alone leave a mark. Still, there are things in the past one has lived through that it is impossible to tell to those who come after.

This book was written at a time when everyone was still in the grip of enthusiasm and nourished by all sorts of illusions; on the other hand, there was plenty to hope for. Even fifteen years ago, however, it might have been a good thing to pause and look at the past before the living memory of it was lost; but anyone who stopped to reflect seemed to have little faith and to want to lag behind. In truth, the future was dark, and if one did not forget the past, it was easy to see it as fatally corruptible. One had only to stop and not be afraid to be taken for a person of little faith, since the gap between hopes and reality made us look like modest prophets. But is there ever anything foreseeable that can still be welcome?

*

For once at least it would be a good idea to give the exact date: *The World Is a Prison* was written in 1945. Those who have spoken of it have generally said 1949, the year of the first Mondadori edition; others, more discerning, said 1948, the year it appeared in the first issue of *Botteghe Oscure*. There have already been other occasions when I thought it would have been better to be specific, but it was something that annoyed me. Besides, the book even says at a certain point: "Finally came the war—which is still going on as I write." The war was still going on.

But there is a private date for the book, I'm pleased to say, and for other reasons: the manuscript was my wedding present to Puci. We were married on 20 September 1945, and so that's its date.

Still, it might not matter much whether it's '45 or '49, but there are those other reasons. At the time, in 1945, the war was not yet over and there was certainly more than the usual room for illusions. With so much enthusiasm in circulation, so many programs, how could we not be swept away, at least a little? Obviously we could have been and even should have been, despite everything. What was possible was possible, if it actually happened to me; one had only to take care that the collective enthusiasms, excellent as they were, not to say useful, did not keep us from remembering what we had inherited; one had to be able to avert one's eyes from the public arena without, however, ignoring it, and go on looking into ourselves as individual realities, and into others as creatures who would again be at the mercy of the incontrovertible human condition. I consider it a more than justified state of mind that made it certain at the time that even many people I esteemed would find the book rather tepid, even, they said, marked by a vague smell of defeatism—just think: certain words were already coming back. But now? Let each make his own reckoning. Yet today I might wish that the last pages in particular had been dictated by the news reports, that they be less true today than then. But instead today they really are.

*

At the time I got out of prison, I hadn't thought much about writing a book. Who knows if I would ever have done so with the notion I had that if we didn't want to lose the flow of ideas, we would have to start again at the point where we'd left off. A few days later, however, I ran into an old friend of mine, a well-known writer; we talked for a while, and I told him a few episodes. "Let's write a book about it together," he said. "I know how these things should be done . . . it will be a great success." No one would have been better at it than he, I was sure of this even then; but at that very moment I had the feeling that what I'd eventually want would be something quite different; with him I wouldn't have succeeded. I found his offer kind, and tried to explain to him why I was turning it down. That same evening I started writing *The World Is a Prison*.

*

The manuscript was ready on 18 September 1945 (but the date is still the other). On the nineteenth I took it to a publisher; I actually had a contract. On returning from a trip I found the proofs ready, I corrected them and waited, but the poor publisher had troubles of his own and shortly went bankrupt. He had helped us in many ways during the hard times, which may be why he failed.

A few months later I found another publisher. Once again I corrected the proofs and waited—and waited. He didn't go bankrupt, but the book didn't come out because he too was waiting. We weren't, however, waiting for the same thing. At first he had been in a great hurry, then he had obviously realized something and persuaded himself that it was better to wait. Certain subjects were already beginning to be less advantageous to some publishers; indeed, those who, like mine, were doing their utmost to interpret the future found them ever more clearly to be avoided. It wasn't they who were mistaken; it was myself, and I too, in my own way, ended by getting rhetorical about it. Who can ever be wholly immune to common evils?

Now that we've seen all kinds of things, including once again swastikas scrawled on walls, one has only to read the newspapers to think that hesitant publishers (to stay with this field) aren't the ones who were mistaken. But it's true that time ends by blaming those who take the easy way out. Fifteen years may steal a life, but they're still a short step.

No need to continue; but at this point, on the same page where last evening I wrote these last lines, I might mention a fact that in some way belies them. It is 3 July, and something has happened in Genoa, something that doesn't contradict, I'd even say confirms, the extent to which the things the postwar period buries every day—but also nourishes, like a fertilizer assisting a slow plant to bloom—go on fermenting underground.

*

By now it made complete sense, the waiting with bankruptcy, the waiting without bankruptcy; I tried, however, to delude myself that it should have been possible to be more discerning. I thought it over, looked around, and decided that, after all, there really was a publisher who functioned where others either failed or hesitated; he was the one the Resistance had hoisted like a banner and that was just what I needed. But no: this time too I had missed the point; there was already more than one "resistance" and mine didn't coincide with his. Therefore, the polite reasons he gave as to why I was not what he had in mind were the same, more or less, as those of other people who later found tepidity and even the smell of defeatism in the pages of my book. So there was no need to go into politics, or even dodge one's own modest professional circle, to comprehend what henceforth was to be the destiny of anyone who recognized the past in extreme "places" and stayed there, where he would also be allowed to be mistaken and correct himself. Nor did it take much to perceive a strange fate reserved for some, that of being chained to a particular rule for having rejected rules.

This was enough to make me do what I didn't, however, do immediately—actually the story of my manuscript went on for a few more months. I think that were I to tell it, it would still preserve the grotesque quality that made me decide to put the book in a drawer, where it would still be, such being my nature, if Princess Caetani had not thought of me on the day she was preparing the first issue of *Botteghe Oscure*.

*

During the first months of war, at a time when the ignorant indifference of youth was being transformed into something that would lead us to accept every eventual responsibility, and which kept being revealed almost automatically to anyone who somehow felt the absurdity of the wartime madness and recognized in it even his own sins of the past decades, among many violent and significant episodes I was somewhat disturbed by a minor event. It was an insignificant and ridiculous one, and even today I can't say for sure why such a thing should stick in my mind.

I was still living in the center of Rome: it's hard to explain how all "those in the center" share a particular sector of life from whose forms and flavor those who do not sleep, eat, work, and play between Largo Chigi and Porta Pinciana, Piazza Venezia and Piazza del Popolo, are excluded. In those days one used to encounter in the streets a tall youth of striking appearance, with one arm in a sling, as I recall, which aroused shock and respect in the passersby. This was something that often happened: some face or other, a person, a couple, generally unknown to the rest of the city, could be a fleeting apparition of which everyone for a while was aware; faces and things that then returned to the anonymity from which they had emerged to give way to other things, other persons, other words or fleeting ideas, arising from who knows where. He was much decorated, a "hero," as well as a momentary hero in the center. His fame was prolonged for a while; *Il Messaggero* took note of his presence, the presence of a war hero side by side on the city sidewalks with ignorant bourgeois types who, for the moment, knew nothing about the war except what they were able to read in the newspapers. I ran into him once while walking with an ardently Fascist friend, who was particularly excited about the epic quality of the times soon to come and was preparing to enlist as a volunteer. Though my friend was fairly tough and also a little blasé, I was struck by his unconcealed agitation and felt some secret chord quivering in him; his whole being was shaken as, not without an awkward eagerness, he pointed the hero out to me: I think "hero" was actually the word he used. Like many, I already knew of his presence "among us," and having seen him before in the streets, bars, or restaurants, had had an indefinable feeling of irritation, not perhaps for the person, who was insignificant, but for the thing, i.e., the myth. I felt uncomfortable and tried to change the subject. Anyway, I would not have given great importance to the matter if I hadn't read a few days later, in the same newspaper that had brought him to the public's attention, that he had been arrested. He was just a nonentity, perhaps a fairly good psychologist, who had found a way to create a brief notoriety for himself and live at his ease, exploiting a fake decoration and attributing to himself a fake wound. He was simply a poor con man. Heroism betrayed really didn't move me; it was during those days that the first news arrived of soldiers dead in the French Alps, and I did not hear any of them described as a hero. What I was unable to forget, however, and which even today remains fixed in my memory with a certain horror, was my friend's unexpected emotional reaction; it gave me the sensation that in people, even those not afflicted with some kind of fanaticism, a dismal and inhuman myth had taken the place of feelings and ideas. Perhaps we have learned in these fifteen years that winning heroes and defeated heroes are the real enemies, the worms that eat away the ground beneath our feet and keep us from comprehending the horror of the truth of all the unheroic dead: millions of dead.

*

By the time *The World Is a Prison* came out as a book, I had already settled on what was inevitable, between my existence, the equivocal postwar period, and that little spark of idealism that my personal experience of the Resistance had caused to grow in my heart. I don't want to go into too much detail; suffice it to say that the last pages of the book were written out of the reality of my situation. Any possibility of my finding a niche for myself had been dispelled, and even those friends who knew me best could do very little to help me. On the contrary, many of them, filled with illusions and theories and exalted expectations, could not understand, and indeed often criticized, what I will call, for lack of a better term, my reluctance.

But in one way or another one must earn one's bread, and so starting in 1948, since I didn't wish to accept certain kinds of employment to which I felt unsuited, I held for more than a year a tiring and unforeseen job, whose hours were between nine in the evening and four in the morning. I worked in the depots of ATAC, the tram company of Rome, where I sat at one of the twenty or thirty windows found in every tram or bus depot, waiting for the trams to arrive at the end of the line. The motormen brought us the day's receipts, and we had to count them, divide the money into piles and rolls, and add up the amounts. It was fairly hard work, under the deafening sheds where the voices, the screech of the rails, the roar of the engines, reminded me vaguely of the few hours spent under the central dome in Regina Cœli before finally getting out. The motormen, tired from their day's work, anxious to return home and go to bed with their wives (this was what they mostly talked about), crowded around the window, swearing and insulting the cashier, who sat immersed in kilos of Allied military lire, tiny Italian paper lire, paper money of every size and description (who now remembers these details of our life then?). I don't know who my colleagues were at the other windows; there were so many of them, and there was quite a turnover.

At a certain hour every night, someone behind us turned on a small radio on the desk of the head cashier; no one listened to it, but it kept us company and perhaps counterbalanced the infernal noise of the shed. It was while counting money, adding up endless figures, that behind me I heard the first comment on my book, which had just then come out. When I realized it, I was afraid one of my coworkers would figure out that the radio was saying something that had to do with me, but it was an absurd worry, I alone knew whom they were talking about, and I may have been the only one there who remembered, albeit with difficulty, my name.

Afterward there were many comments on *The World Is a Prison,* perhaps too many; but I was less interested in the reviews than in the letters that came to me from various sides. I noticed they were mostly from individuals of the generation older than mine or from young people, and as a result I had to admit that even the most welcome letters did not contain the one observation I was waiting for. I was not entirely disappointed, since a few of my contemporaries also wrote me, but only Vasco was able to express in words something that was more important to me than any praise or agreement. In his letter, he wrote the following judgment, one I had been expecting and the only one I cared about: "You've written for all of us (we who are more or less your age and who write) the words that should have been written about us. From the most unexpected position and perhaps for that very reason the most morally lucid one, you have 'accounted for' a generation of intellectuals. . . ." It was a fine letter and I kept it. There were also remarks and opinions that we've had a chance to discuss over the years, but the sentence I'd been waiting for was that one, and even though it came to me from only one of my contemporaries, it was enough for me because it was all I asked—not perhaps without a bit of immodesty, but that doesn't matter.

*

During that difficult trip from Rome to Lucca, a small occurrence in a truck, where I found myself with two soldiers and another person whom I'm unable to recall, left a fairly deep mark in my memories, though I neglected to write about it. We were halfway between Civitavecchia and Tarquinia; despite bright sunshine, it was cold on the open truck, and we suffered from the wind. After taking a pack of cigarettes out of my suitcase and offering it around— inside I had seven more packs—I closed my eyes and it must have looked as though I was sleeping. For a while the two soldiers kept checking my immobility; then, doubtless convinced I was asleep, they opened the suitcase with their hands behind their backs, took out a pack of cigarettes for each, and skillfully and stealthily closed it again, sighing with relief at a successful operation. I saw it all and remember even the slightest details. I remained motionless, however, gripped by an exaggerated concern that I might involuntarily betray myself. The very thought that I might have risen up in protest gave me a curious feeling: I was ashamed. I didn't move until I was absolutely sure that the two soldiers could no longer suspect that I had seen.

Actually, the two soldiers were not guilty of anything; rather, they were obeying the logic of their situation, of the absurd years that had put them with me onto that truck, brutally beaten and deprived of everything. I knew very well that had I intervened it would have been enough to appeal to the law of respect for the property of others for them to feel ashamed and agree with me about their guilt. But the guilty one would certainly have been myself, as indeed I was, and I was ashamed of it. So many times in the past fifteen years we have had to be secretly ashamed of the misunderstandings and mistakes of others. To place oneself on the side of the elect, those who were right, and put others in the wrong does nothing but add to the emotional confusion. We are all guilty, as I increasingly learned, especially when those who, logically speaking, should have been completely right arrived in our midst, and we had to realize that they too carried the inevitable baggage of guilt. But this is an argument that goes too far beyond my present purpose, and really belongs to the historian, if anything in our news reports may be called history.

*

I would have liked to have a little conversation with this book, private and detached, but that doesn't seem possible. Just now when I wanted to immerse myself in a few pages of notes for reasons all my own, what is going on around me seems to want to interfere, and seems to be of the same nature as the things I wished to say. Today, 8 July, five people have died in Reggio Emilia. What does all this mean? Are they still dying for the same reasons for which so many died, the same reasons for which I too was in danger of losing my life when I was a little over thirty? It looks that way. But actually everything has changed, a shadow hangs over these episodes in which that emotional confusion, the horror of which we have been enduring for so long, recurs. But even the dead in Reggio Emilia, these five, surely lie outside the news reports that attack or uphold their sacrifice; they too are dead like many I myself saw: this one must believe.

*

I had tried several times before, but had lost patience; this time, on the road between Livorno and Pisa, I was able to recognize the house where I had stopped the night after Christmas. I didn't approach it because someone would surely have asked me why; it was enough to recognize it from the road, and it looked to me as though little or nothing had changed. In Pisa, on the other hand, I tried to view the Arno embankment again from the same perspective as before; then I had seen only destruction and was not able to see it that way again. The fact is that even old buildings still standing with no sign of reconstruction had looked destroyed to me. I had been so tired when I got there.

Almost inadvertently, I also sought out the point at which Lucca, from the road that descends the mountain, can be seen below with its towers emerging from the greenery of the trees on its walls. Here, indeed, not only did I rediscover the image, but also my previous emotion. Again I saw this island, locked in the heart of Tuscany and resembling nothing in its surroundings, this conformist place where real life is a secret that is kept under wraps, this magic circle in which I now feel myself a stranger. It's Rome's fault, of course, the city I love and which has made me an orphan, depriving me of ancestral ties and early affections, like a woman who steals a father from his children and legitimate family and holds him, extinguishing remorse and the raison d'être of old affections in a sinful exuberance he cannot do without. There is no poison in my life that Rome does not share; I derive no joy from Rome that does not smell bitter and harsh, or that does not arouse my awareness through something that feels like sin, even if it is the kind of sin by which, and only by which, one glimpses with brutal lucidity the best way to save oneself.

*

In the book I omitted everything about Carlo C., all the things he told me every day. I did so deliberately; he was a character out of place in the cells of Via Tasso. He was there because he had killed a German, but the reasons for his act had nothing to do with political ideals or resentment: to him, the man he killed was someone who was interfering with his illicit deals. And yet Carlo was a character of singular strength; being accustomed to prison, even under these circumstances, he was sure of himself, prompt and steady, and not lacking in defiance. His attitude toward the others was one of superiority, and only with me, as he was kind enough to say, did he feel at ease. He even told me I was made of the right stuff, and that when we got out of there we might see each other again. "There's no limit," he said, "to our solidarity. At the most critical moment in my life, I went to New York without a passport, in the hold of a freighter. I was able to leave the waterfront and meet colleagues who solved all my problems in twenty-four hours, including money. All I had to do was sit quietly drinking in a certain bar, and all day long everyone was working for my benefit, to supply me with dollars, take care of certain matters, and send me back home the same way I'd come. That's what I call solidarity. In Naples, of course, I have to do the same for anyone who finds himself in the same situation there. That's solidarity!" No one contradicted him. Me, whom he considered to be a man of quality, he advised: "If you don't know where to find me when we get out of here, come to Naples. Go to the waterfront and ask for the Captain—that's me and everybody knows me. We'll see that you get whatever you need. I have only to say the word and you'll be able to walk around Naples like a boss, respected by everybody. Come to Naples, we see that nobody gets in trouble." I never asked who he meant by "we," but he had all the air of knowing that I had no difficulty in understanding. On one of the last days, before they parted us, he sought to give me more confidential instructions: "Even in Rome you'll be able to get in touch with me; go to such and such a street, So-and-so's fabric store, and ask for the Captain." A few weeks after the arrival of the Allies, I actually went to the store he mentioned, a fairly important store on a downtown street. I asked one of the salesgirls for the Captain and had hardly finished the sentence when two individuals came out of the back of the store with, shall we say, rather fierce scowls on their faces. "Who are you?" they asked. I explained, and they looked at each other for a moment, then replied brusquely, with a studied vehemence that effectively put an end to our conversation: "We don't know the Captain, good-bye." I left with some apprehension and I daresay rather quickly. Later I was often in Naples, but my curiosity no longer got the better of me; I would have been afraid—even afraid, why not say it, of myself.

*

It was possible to create for oneself a tough inner isolation, a habit of mind that would help in enduring prison, even the one on Via Tasso, without losing control of one's feelings. It's a matter of structures that are highly resistant until they are attacked by elements too unexpected or too close to what has been excluded. I had succeeded in this, but there was a moment when it all came crashing down, or at least it seemed to, since I recovered it immediately thereafter intact, the whole protective edifice in which I rigorously intended to live. It was during the transfer from Via Tasso to Regina Cœli: the truck drove across the city and, for better or worse, I was again seeing the streets, and the people on the sidewalks going about their everyday affairs. Of course, the city was different, everywhere there was a gloomy and suspect air; but having just left a place that still today seems unreal to me, I was struck by how absurd it was that everything outside should proceed according to a more or less usual and normal order. It was a painful image, but a tolerable one; toward Largo Chigi, however, I had a glimpse of Libero crossing the street behind three armed Germans, engrossed, his shoulders drooping a little, and more in a hurry than usual; he may have been on his way to his favorite trattoria. It was a moment of unwitting joy that threatened to ruin me and smash the terrible equilibrium that I defended with a certain ferocity: I had seen a friend again, and for a moment had been immersed in the lost world. It was the last familiar image; it had been brushed against unawares, struck by my vehement, voiceless appeal, then unknowingly lost in the streets of the city. He would never know of it, and for me it had surely been the last opportunity to yearn toward a friendly being, toward a world no longer mine.

*

That passage that begins "So are prison and freedom not real prison, real freedom?" has been quoted too many times and commented on too often, but to tell the truth, not according to the meaning that ought to be given to these words: perhaps people gladly quote whatever lends itself to being taken the way they would wish it. Actually these are simple and spontaneous words, and were not intended to go beyond their obscure bitterness: it would be better not to be born, since often there are no solutions to the human condition; the world is a prison whose dimensions do not change the impossibility of overstepping the barriers of life. I had already seen all too well that my second thoughts did not come from anything real.

In this connection, my first reviewer spoke of one of my "second thoughts." We discussed it when we met and got to know each other; we decided to see each other again to talk about it all. He died before we could meet again; too bad, because I knew what I would have liked to say to him on this subject, I had gone over it in my mind, and with his death was almost deprived of any chance to say it.

It was not a second thought in the sense that even Pancrazi* had expressed in his piece, but something both more and less. More than once I had seen death a few hours away, and I think I can say that one can go to meet one's end, when one knows it to be real, not only without regret for all the things one leaves behind, but also without the feeling that being born is only an accident. It's an opportunity, and anyone who does not neglect it, and seizes it as best he can, is far from thinking that an adventure is ending. I had had need of a heroic spirit, a human composure useful only to myself, and from this I learned, and continue

*The critic Pietro Pancrazi wrote a preface to the 1949 Mondadori edition of *The World Is a Prison.*—Trans.

to learn, that it's possible to believe in endless "imitations" of perfection.

*

Those who met me when I was twenty, or let's say twenty-five, would have had no difficulty in noticing how sure I was of having had a lot of experience; it may seem puerile to think of it today, but it's true, and I would have plenty of arguments to prove it. Those who meet me today, friends who meet me insofar as I put myself out, will find me rather naive, almost boyish in nature: this too is certainly true. I have not, however, given up anything I was able to get from life; perhaps I have only ended by learning that the wider the picture of your experiences becomes, the more the background of reality against which they must be seen expands: the more you find, the more you lose.

So far I have no desire whatsoever to evade any appeal that might once again arouse my conscience; but today when the maturity of my years is finally a boon to me, when I know the look of the things we had to face in order to become men and give what we could to "everyday life," I reject all illusions: one acquires the rights of age only with time, which otherwise has been wasted. Once you have come to perceive that you now act knowing the extent of your possible indifference, you have also come to know, without especially caring, that of all the people of your acquaintance, perhaps less than one in a thousand will not be mistaken about what you are.

The things we have reconciled best with reality are those that in memory have been confused with the imagination: indeed, a spontaneous sentiment of human solidarity is more imaginative and fruitful than an abstract, fanciful combination of colors. Among those who profess social solidarity, I long did my utmost to find one who would communicate to me the secret of his mission; I lost a lot of time trying to discover a sign of anxiety, a spontaneous grief, in the many champions of one's fellow man. None succeeded in convincing me that he knew whether one or a hundred thousand oppressed and desperate people had a face.

There are some experiences hard to destroy when one's small fund of knowledge has been exposed to all storms. What one felt two days ago looking at a photograph that showed a poor black man with calm eyes being struck by two colonialists, their brutal faces obsessed with violence, is worth much more than anything written in the books and actions of all the administrators of people's rights and freedoms.

With all this, until an outlet comes along in the shape of some general agreement, and I myself risk turning into a respectable champion, I must add that I am better able to get along with a misfit who understands and bears the weight of his own destiny than with those good souls who are able to adapt themselves to tested ideas, albeit of common sense and public morality. I now have more faith in someone who is able to doubt himself than in those who know all about what needs to be done.

Those who knew me when I was young found a man who had suffered, like many for that matter, who believed in his own ideas and held them worthy of any sacrifice; those who know me now find a man who is not afraid to appear to be lacking, still capable perhaps of self-sacrifice, but no longer able to believe wholly in the object of his sacrifices. The space in which I have found the things of my life has grown ever larger to the extent that they have grown, until the world around me has become so wide that by now they have turned out to be a speck of dust.